ACROSS OUR GREAT N/
LEGAL NUTCASES A

In Fort Madison, Iowa, the fire departmer
tice fire-fighting techniques for 15 minutes be   ....g any fire. (44)

In Kansas, a former insurance official hurt himself trying to lift his briefcase from his car trunk. Even though he didn't miss any time on the job—or even his golf game—he was awarded $95,000 for a work-related injury. (7)

In Margate City, New Jersey, it is illegal to surf in the nude or with a sock over the male genitals. (25)

In Whitehall, Montana, you can't drive a truck or car with ice picks attached to the wheels. (163)

In Nashua, New Hampshire, a teenage basketball player went up for a slam dunk and got more hang time than Michael Jordan: His teeth caught in the net on the way down. His parents sued the net maker for his dental repairs—and won. (159)

COLLECTED FROM COURT RECORDS AND OTHER OFFICIAL
SOURCES, OR SWORN ON A STACK OF BIBLES, THESE RIOTOUS
RULINGS, LUDICROUS LEGAL PROCEEDINGS, AND MORE ARE
UNAUTHORIZED AND UNBELIEVABLY HILARIOUS!

Also by the author

GREAT GOVERNMENT GOOFS!
AMERICA'S DUMBEST CRIMINALS

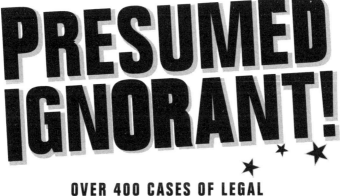

PRESUMED IGNORANT!

OVER 400 CASES OF LEGAL LOONINESS, DAFFY DEFENDANTS, AND BLOOPERS FROM THE BENCH

LELAND H. GREGORY III

A DELL TRADE PAPERBACK

A DELL TRADE PAPERBACK

Published by
Dell Publishing
a division of
Bantam Doubleday Dell Publishing Group, Inc.
1540 Broadway
New York, New York 10036

Library of Congress Cataloging in Publication Data

Gregory, Leland H.
    Presumed ignorant! : over 400 cases of legal looniness, daffy defendants, and bloopers from the bench / Leland H. Gregory III.
    p.   cm.
    ISBN 0-440-50789-8
    1. Law—United States—Humor.   I. Title.
K184.G744   1998
349.73'02'07—dc21   97-44905
                                                                         CIP

Printed in the United States of America

Published simultaneously in Canada

August 1998

10 9 8 7 6 5 4 3 2 1

BVG

This book, along with my heart, is dedicated to my wife, Gloria. Thank you for your patience, love, encouragement, and advice, and for giving me the most beautiful son imaginable.

ACKNOWLEDGMENTS

People do foolish things. Every day we see examples of someone else's foolishness; hopefully we've learned it's not polite to point—I, however, never learned that little piece of etiquette. As long as people continue to do foolish things, I'll continue to point my finger at them. This book isn't intended to be a slam against the legal system; well, sort of, but not completely. Since the legal system is composed of people, I'm simply pointing out the human folly in the field of law. There are a lot of good things about our judicial system—but that wouldn't make a very funny book, would it?

The author would like to personally thank the American Tort Reform Association for their invaluable information and the American Bar Association for their sense of humor and fair dealing.

I would like to thank my wife, Gloria Graves Gregory, for her comments, edits, and suggestions on the manuscript; and to my friend Barry McAlister, who helped me uncover some hard-to-find research. A special thanks to my agent, Jonathon Lazear, and all the wonderful people at the Lazear Agency, and to Kathleen Jayes, my editor at Dell, who also came up with the title for this book.

I would also like to thank the men and women who got caught up in our legal system and wound up earning a place in this book.

Ho, Ho, Hee, Hee

It's a serious case. A federal lawsuit. The Wawa food-store chain, which controls 500 outlets in five states, is demanding that the lone HAHA market in eastern Pennsylvania change its name. In their lawsuit filed in late 1996, Wawa claims that HAHA is too similar in sound and could confuse people into believing that HAHA is affiliated with Wawa. HAHA owners Tamilee and George Haaf, Jr., claim they have a right to use the name since it is simply an abbreviation of their last name. They originally considered "Haaf and Haaf" as the name of their market, but settled on HAHA instead. Wawa claims that HAHA's defense is poo-poo.

An ordinance in Grangeville, Idaho, reads: "No citizen shall allow their turkeys, chickens, cattle, horses, lions, or tigers to be led by chains along a street in this community."

A Devil of a Lawsuit

On the day before Halloween, a lawyer from Little Rock, Arkansas, decided to file a federal class action suit to stop public schools from observing the "rites and customs and practices of the religion of Satan on its annual high unholy day." The case is listed as: *Forbes, All Christian Children, Their Parents, Taxpayers of Arkansas, Jesus Christ, Lord, Savior, Best Friend, Master, King of Kings & Rightful Sovereign vs. Department of Education, School District, School Board, High Priests of Secular Humanism, Communist Party USA, Church of Satan, the Anti-Christs, Satan, the God of this World System.* Everyone thought it was going to be an uncontested lawsuit until, surprisingly, Satan filed a motion to dismiss the suit. Another Little Rock lawyer, John Wesley Hall, playing the devil's advocate, claimed that Satan couldn't be sued because he lacked sufficient "minimum contacts" with the state of Arkansas to allow a suit in a federal court. In this case, "minimum contacts" meant that Satan had never transacted business, owned property, written contracts, or filed any other lawsuit in Arkansas. The case was dismissed. Thank God.

"Burglars are prohibited from entering or leaving the scene of a crime by the front door."
—*a Lincoln, Nebraska, ordinance*

America's Saddest Home Video

In 1993, 26-year-old Cleophus "Little Pie" Prince, Jr., was standing trial in San Diego for the murder of six women. In order to better convey the tragedy of the death of one of the victims to the jurors, the prosecutor played a videotape showing the young woman, an aspiring actress, during performances and at home. Emotions ran high during the videotape showing; there wasn't a dry eye in the house. Among those crying the loudest and most inconsolably was Prince's own attorney. Since Prince's attorney was moved to tears, the judge moved for a recess. When the jury returned to the courtroom, they returned with a guilty verdict. Prince was later sentenced to be executed. Who's crying now?

**It is against the law in Kentucky
to throw eggs at a public speaker.**

Moon Over Idaho

University of Idaho freshman Jason Wilkins thought it would be funny to "moon" his friends from a third-story dormitory window. The 18-year-old climbed on top of a three-foot-high radiator, dropped his pants, and pressed his butt against the window, which promptly shattered. Wilkins suffered four fractured vertebrae, abrasions to his hands, and a "deeply bruised buttocks" from the fall. After he picked himself up off the concrete, the embarrassed Wilkins said, "This is just a freak accident." But six months after the accident, Wilkins had a change of heart. He and his parents sued school officials, claiming they were negligent for failing to warn dorm residents of "the danger associated with upper-story windows." They asked for $940,000 in damages—that's $470,000 per cheek, in case you were wondering. The claim was denied. "We've got a kid that's presumably of average intelligence with his bare bottom against a window, leaning back," said Al Campbell, claims manager for the state's Bureau of Risk Management. "That doesn't seem very bright to me."

Tightrope walking is outlawed everywhere in Winchester, Massachusetts—except in church.

A Poor Excuse for an Excuse

Before insurance companies release a dime for any accident, they check the motorist's statements given at the time of the accident. Understandably, motorists are sometimes confused following an accident and meaning to say something isn't always saying what you mean . . . if you know what I mean. Here are actual explanations from insurance company forms written by motorists, first published in the *Toronto Sun* on July 26, 1977.

- "I thought my window was down but found it up when I put my head through it."

- "The guy was all over the road. I had to swerve a number of times before I hit him."

- "I had been driving my car for 40 years when I fell asleep at the wheel and had an accident."

- "To avoid hitting the bumper of the car in front, I struck the pedestrian."

- "I told the police that I was not injured, but on removing my hat, I found that I had a skull fracture."

- "The pedestrian had no idea what direction to go, so I ran over him."

- "I saw the slow-moving, sad-faced old gentleman as he bounced off my car."

- "I was thrown from my car as I left the road. I was later found in a ditch by some stray cows."

- "I was unable to stop in time and my car crashed into the other vehicle. The driver and passengers then left immediately for a vacation with injuries."

An ordinance in Oklahoma reads: "The driver of any vehicle involved in an accident resulting in death shall immediately stop and give his name and address to the person struck."

Lawyers You Love to Hate

- A former insurance official in Kansas hurt himself trying to lift his briefcase from his car trunk. Even though he missed no work or even a golf game on account of the injury, he was awarded $95,000 because of the work-related injury.

- A law firm in New Orleans routinely billed four hours of work for letters that were only one sentence in length.

- A Chicago lawyer charged $25,000 for "ground transportation" while on business in San Francisco.

- A Kansas lawyer received nearly $35,000 in workmen's compensation because he hurt his shoulder reaching into the backseat of his car for his briefcase.

- One lawyer, while working on a government contract, wrote a definition of the words "and/or" that was over 300 words in length.

The Virginia legislature passed a law in 1658 outlawing lawyers. In case you're wondering, it's no longer on the books.

That Little Rascal

In 1993 the Maryland Supreme Court suspended Easton attorney George J. Goldsborough, Jr., for his rather heavy-handed approach to disciplining employees and clients. Goldsborough's former secretary testified that "approximately once a week" over the course of her 21 months of employment—a total of nearly 84 times—Goldsborough would spank her for making typographical errors. One of Goldsborough's ex-partners said he found a copy of the book *Spanking and the Single Girl* in Goldsborough's desk. And a former client testified under oath that Goldsborough "told her she was a bad girl, pulled her over his knee and spanked her lightly several times" when she came to him for legal advice.

When the proceedings were over, the supreme court concluded: "An attorney of Goldsborough's experience and capabilities should reasonably be expected to know that spanking one's secretary will not be tolerated." Goldsborough was then banned from practicing law (he had been an active member of the Maryland Bar Association for 42 years). In his own defense, Goldsborough argued that he shouldn't be punished because what he did "was not strictly law-related." Colleagues of Goldsborough's were criticized for not acting against Goldsborough sooner. Rumors of Goldsborough's open-handed form of discipline were so widespread that his law firm was referred to as "Spanky and the Gang." ➡

In Pacific Grove, California, according to City Ordinance No. 352, it is a misdemeanor to kill or threaten a butterfly.

Beauty Is Only Skin Deep

The City of Big Shoulders, a.k.a. Chicago, Illinois, is the only city known to have an "Ugly Law." It states: "No person who is diseased, maimed, mutilated or in any way deformed so as to be an unsightly or disgusting object, or an improper person to be allowed in or on the public ways or other public places in this city, shall therein or thereon expose himself to public view, under a penalty of not less than $1 nor more than $50 for each offense."

It is against the law in New Jersey to slurp soup in a public restaurant.

You Dirty Rat

When Frank Balun went out into his New Jersey garden on a warm summer's day in July 1993 to check on his tomato vines, he discovered some of the tomato plants had been eaten by rats. Balun was incensed. He set out a series of traps to catch the felonious furry creatures. During the night he heard a trap spring; he found a rat alive in the trap and killed it. Soon the Associated Humane Societies in Newark filed charges against Balun for needlessly killing the rat. They complained that instead of murdering the rotund rodent, Balun should have dealt with it more humanely. In 1994 Municipal Court Judge Albert Parsonnel ruled that there was a statutory exception which allows people to kill vermin which destroy crops or livestock. Even though the evidence against the rat was circumstantial—there were no witnesses, and the rat wasn't discovered in the act of eating the tomatoes—the judge exonerated Balun and dismissed the charges. In case you're wondering, the judge's ruling eliminated any chance of the rat's family filing a wrongful death lawsuit against Balun.

It is against the law in Seattle, Washington, for goldfish in a bowl to ride a city bus unless the fish are kept still.

The Prison Files Part 1

In the old days, prisoners tried to escape the confines of their cell by using a file hidden inside a cake. Today, thanks to our criminal justice system, prisoners try to escape their boredom by filing a lawsuit, which *is* a piece of cake. Because inmates are considered "indigent," they don't have to pay filing fees and are either given a court-appointed lawyer or can represent themselves. Every claim, no matter how frivolous, must be considered by the district attorney's office. Over 90 percent of prisoner cases are determined frivolous and therefore dismissed.

● Glenn Spradley, who is serving a life sentence for attempted murder and aggravated assault in Florida, sued for three pancakes instead of two.

● Michael A. Johnson, who was serving time in Lorton Reformatory filed a lawsuit for $12,500 because he was charged $6 for a $5.80 book of postage stamps. A federal judge in Washington, D.C., dismissed the lawsuit.

● A lawsuit was filed against Buchanan County, Missouri, alleging that the county should award damages to a prisoner who broke his leg while attempting to escape from its jail.

It is against the law in Salt Lake City, Utah, to carry an unwrapped ukulele on the street.

Shooting Holes in the Law

Forty-two-year-old Eugene Baylis entered a local biker bar in Colorado Springs, armed with an AK-47 automatic rifle, four hand grenades, a pistol, and a flak jacket. Several patrons, seeing the heavily armed Baylis, advanced to try and stop him from doing anything rash. Baylis felt threatened by their approach and opened fire, killing two people and injuring five. When the shooting spree was over, Baylis was arrested and charged with first-degree murder and attempted murder. The public defender assigned to the case argued that Baylis had gone to the biker bar merely to look for a man who had shot him with a pellet gun earlier in the day. The public defender claimed Baylis had been planning simply to hold the air-gun attacker until the police arrived—but when he had been accosted by the patrons in the bar, he had had no choice but to shoot them dead . . . in self-defense, of course. The jury apparently thought this made a lot of sense; it found Baylis not guilty on all counts. One of the jurors said the prosecution didn't prove Baylis had had any real intentions of killing anyone when he had entered the bar and "didn't disprove that he acted in self-defense." How dare the patrons in the bar assume that just because someone walks in carrying an assault rifle, hand grenades, and a handgun, that he plans to do anything other than have a beer or a quick shot.

**It is illegal to spit against the wind in
Sault Sainte Marie, Michigan.**

Rain, Rain, Go Away—and That's an Order!

U.S. District Court Judge Samuel King was weary of jurors not showing up because of the heavy rains that plagued California during the early part of 1986. He decreed: "I hereby order that it cease raining by Tuesday." Shortly after this declaration, the rain stopped—and five years of severe drought fell upon California. In February 1991 Judge King proclaimed, "I hereby rescind my order of February 18, 1986, and order that rain shall fall in California beginning February 27, 1991." Later that same day, February 27, 1991, Californians saw four inches of rain, the greatest accumulation in a decade. The judge claimed this sudden change in the weather was "proof positive that we are a nation governed by laws." From then on, no one has brought a cloud around to rain on Judge King's parade.

In the city of Stark, Kansas, it is against the law to quack like a duck.

A Case of O. J.

Several cases during this century have been dubbed "The Trial of the Century." Among them are: *People v. Richard Loeb and Nathan Leopold* (a.k.a. the Leopold & Loeb trial), *Commonwealth v. Nicola Sacco and Bartolomeo Vanzetti* (a.k.a. the Sacco & Vanzetti trial), *State v. John T. Scopes* (a.k.a. the Scopes Monkey trial), and *People v. Bruno Richard Hauptmann* (a.k.a. the Lindbergh Baby kidnapping). But without a doubt, the most famous trial of recent times has been *People v. O. J. Simpson* (1995). O. J. Simpson has become a part of American folklore—but at what cost? Take a look:

$3.6 million to investigate and prosecute the case
$3 million in food, security, and shelter for the jury
$2.7 million in Sheriff's department expenses
$1.9 million in court costs (superior and municipal)
$100,000 for autopsies
$21,000 in accounting costs

And an estimated $40 billion in loss of productivity due to American workers discussing the Simpson trial instead of doing their job.

Cuts right to the heart of the matter, doesn't it?

A Seattle, Washington, law specifies the legal limit on the length of any concealed weapon which one may carry. The weapon can be no more than six feet long.

Sometimes Justice Is Blind

In February 1995 the Texas State Commission on Judicial Conduct publicly reprimanded Judge J. R. "Bob" Musslewhite of Harris County after it uncovered that, while serving as a judge, Musslewhite apparently made overt sexual remarks to a female prosecutor in 1992, and during 1992 and 1993 touched the buttocks of another female prosecutor, as well as a female intern. The commission also discovered that in early 1993 Musslewhite had gulped down the liquor, which had been admitted into evidence in a DUI case, saying to the prosecutor, "I'm glad you lost so I don't have to preserve the evidence." And to top it all off, in December 1993 Judge Musslewhite, while adjudicating a drunk-driving case, was seen drinking beer while the jury was in deliberation. The commission concluded, "For a judge to consume alcohol and preside while under the effects of alcohol during trials of alcohol-related offenses brings scorn and disrespect to the judiciary." I'll drink to that!

Children riding on a train are not allowed to drink milk while passing through the state of North Carolina.

A Bird on the "Wing-Ding"

In February 1995 attorney Charles Peruto, Jr., was negotiating a low bail for his client in a Norristown, Pennsylvania, courtroom. Even though his client, Howard "Wing Ding" Jones, was an accused drug dealer, Peruto tried to convince the judge that his client would not jump bail. The judge didn't believe Peruto's argument and raised Jones's bail from $1,000 to $150,000—at which point Jones fled the courtroom. A wing-a-ding-ding and away we go!

It is "unlawful to tease or torment skunks or polecats" in Minnesota.

All or Bust

Richard Osborn walked into Emporium Videos and found just the video he was looking for. The cover of the adult video, "Belle of the Ball" advertised that it starred the well-endowed actress Busty Belle. But when Osborn got home, he discovered that Ms. Belle only appeared in approximately eight to nine minutes of the 60-plus minute X-rated video. Did he do what any red-blooded American male would do—rewind the tape and watch it again? No! He sued. Osborn's lawsuit sought $29.95 for the cost of the video, $55.79 in medical expenses for the asthma attack he had suffered because of the "stress and strain of being ripped off," and $50,000 for "pain and suffering." (What had caused him "pain and suffering" isn't clear—and I don't think I want to know, anyway.) The Natrona County, Wyoming, District Court originally dismissed the complaint stating that it contained no cause for action. But in March 1993, the Wyoming Supreme Court revived Osborn's claim on the grounds that he should have been given a chance to challenge the dismissal. Chief Justice Richard Macy, who disagreed with the other supreme court judges, said, "The facts of Osborn's case simply cannot be forged into a claim. It is crystal clear that the real culprit was Osborn's endogenous salaciousness." In other words, Osborn's trust went bust because his lust for bust went bust. And thus, his suit was moot.

**There is a law in Kingman, Arizona, which prohibits
all camel hunting within the city limits.**

Divorce American Style

Nearly 50 percent of all marriages in the United States end in divorce. Most of the time the cause is something as vague as "irreconcilable differences." But sometimes the reasons for divorcing are more specific. Here are some examples:

- A man in Tarittville, Connecticut, filed for divorce because his wife left him a note on the refrigerator which read: "I won't be home when you return from work. Have gone to the bridge club. There'll be a recipe for your dinner at 7 o'clock on Channel 2."

- A man in Hazard, Kentucky, divorced his wife because she "beat him whenever he removed onions from his hamburger without first asking for permission."

- The South Dakota Supreme Court upheld a divorce court ruling in September 1994, citing the husband as the cause of the couple's troubles. The husband had, among other bad habits, a tendency of passing gas around the house and then getting angry with his wife when she complained. The wife claimed her husband could easily regulate his odoriferous emissions and would break wind as a "retaliation thing."

- A man in Long Island filed for divorce against his wife claiming that she is a witch and routinely practices ritualistic animal sacrifices.

- A deaf man in Bennettsville, South Carolina, filed for divorce because his wife "was always nagging him in sign language."

- A woman in Canon City, Colorado, divorced her husband because he forced her to "duck under the dashboard whenever they drove past his girlfriend's house."

- A woman in Hardwick, Georgia, divorced her husband on the grounds that he "stayed home too much and was much too affectionate."

It is strictly forbidden in Los Angeles, California, to bathe two babies in the same tub at the same time.

Full Circle Rehabilitation

In November 1973 prosecutor William Lawler of Madison County, Indiana, won his case for the county against 18-year-old Rodney Cummings on burglary charges. The judge sentenced Cummings to three years' probation and then apparently Lawler helped young Cummings see the light. Cummings joined the Anderson Police Department, made detective and eventually became a lawyer himself. Was Lawler pleased? Not really. In the November 1994 elections, in a close race, Cummings beat Lawler out of his job and became Madison County's new prosecuting attorney. What goes around comes around.

It is against the law in Louisiana to rob a bank and then shoot at a bank teller with a water pistol.

Reading, 'Riting, and 'Rithmatic

In 1995 Connecticut Judge Socrates Mihalakos ruled that Nancy Sekor, a middle-school teacher who had been fired from her job in 1993 for incompetence, had to be reinstated. His reasoning? Sekor had been judged incompetent in only two of the three subjects she taught.

An ordinance in Dallas, Texas, forbids "walking about aimlessly, without apparent purpose, lingering, hanging around, lagging behind, idly spending time, delaying, sauntering and moving slowly about."

Surprise Attack

Timothy Hudson, a Florida native, broke into a house he thought was empty. He was burglarizing the place when he discovered a woman was home. He pulled out a knife, stabbed her to death, and dumped her body in a drainage ditch. When he went to trial, the jury found him guilty and sentenced him to death; it was a clear case of murder. Florida Supreme Court Judge Rosemary Barkett didn't see it so clearly, however. When the case came before her on appeal in the mid-1980s, Judge Barkett voted against the death penalty conviction. She reasoned that since Hudson hadn't believed the woman to be home, her sudden appearance had been so shocking to Hudson that he hadn't had time to weigh his options, and so he had killed her. The judge ruled that Hudson "was apparently surprised by the victim during his burglarizing of the home [and thus] unable to conform his conduct to the requirements of law." If Hudson is ever released, I hope no one is stupid enough to throw him a surprise coming-home party.

A Boston, Massachusetts, ordinance states: "A lodger shall not be lodged for more than seven consecutive nights unless he shall have taken a bath."

Wright Is Wright

In June 1993 an Army sergeant won a court order in Maryland to legally have his name changed. The next day he had second thoughts and went before a judge to get his original name back. But the Anne Arundel Circuit Court judge informed the sergeant-formally-known-as-Tyrone-Victor-Wright that he would have a 30-day wait before he could use his original name again. So for the next month, Tyrone Victor Wright was called by his new name, Jesus Christ Hallelujah. The newly christened Mr. Hallelujah told the judge he was having second thoughts about the name change after speaking with his family. "We're all happy with Tyrone Victor Wright," he said. Hallelujah!

"Since the Jasper husband is accountable for his wife's misbehavior, he has the legal right to chastise her with a stick no larger around than his thumb."
—*a Jasper, Alabama, ordinance*

Nights in White Satin

It is one of the only prisoner-filed lawsuits that ever worked out best for the taxpayers. David Earl Dempsey, then 37, an inmate at the Pima County jail in Arizona, filed a lawsuit against prison officials in February 1996 seeking damages for a botched suicide attempt. Dempsey claimed the guards and other officials were negligent in allowing him to have bed sheets in his cell which he used to tie around his neck and jump out a jail window. Obviously Dempsey wasn't a Boy Scout because the knot he tied in the sheet unraveled and he plummeted to the concrete below, injuring himself. Before the case could appear before a judge, Dempsey saved the court and the taxpayers money by attempting suicide a second time and succeeding. In a situation like this I feel compelled to quote, "If at first you don't succeed . . ."

In Margate City, New Jersey, it is illegal to surf in the nude or with a sock over the male genitals.

Gee, He Must Be a Knotzy

Charged with strangling a Fort Lauderdale, Florida, prostitute, Donald Leroy Evans wanted a little respect. Evans, then 38, filed a motion which would allow him to wear a Ku Klux Klan robe during his court appearance. The motion also requested that Evans's name be officially changed on all court documents to "the honorable and respected name of Hi Hitler." Apparently, Evans thought Hitler's subjects were chanting "Hi Hitler" instead of "Heil, Hitler." I wonder if anyone had the heart to tell him the Nazis didn't refer to Hitler as "Mine Fewer," either.

It is illegal in Carmel, California, for a woman to take a bath in a business office.

Rhyme and Reason

Judge John H. Gillis and two other judges of the Michigan Appellate Court were faced with an interesting lawsuit in which $15,000 was demanded for the pain and suffering—of a tree. The driver of an automobile collided with the plaintiff's "beautiful oak" and severely damaged its bark. The driver paid the tree owner $550 for a tree surgeon to help spruce up the tree, but the owner wanted more. Judge Gillis couldn't see how a tree could be compensated for pain and suffering so he rejected the demand, but he was so overcome by the tree's majesty that he penned his decision in rhyme. The court rendered its decision in *Fisher v. Lowe* (Mich. Ct. App. 1983) as follows:

> *We thought that we would never see*
> *A suit to compensate a tree.*
> *A suit whose claim in tort is prest*
> *Upon a mangled tree's behest;*
> *A tree whose battered trunk was prest*
> *Against a Chevy's crumpled crest;*
> *A tree that faces each new day*
> *With bark and limb in disarray;*
> *A tree that may forever bear*
> *A lasting need for loving care.*
> *Flora lovers though we three,*
> *We must uphold the court's decree.*
> *Affirmed.*

At least the judge didn't get too sappy.

"Two vehicles which are passing each other in opposite directions shall have the right of way."
—*New York State Vehicle and Traffic Law Article 6, Paragraph 82, Subsection Division 3*

Perry Mason Lives!

In a Houston, Texas, courtroom in April 1994, Arthur Hollingsworth was on trial for the armed robbery of a convenience store. Hollingsworth waived his constitutional right to remain silent and testified in his own defense. Harris County prosecutor Jay Hileman eventually got Hollingsworth to admit he was, in fact, in the Sun Mart convenience store at the time of the holdup. Hileman then got Hollingsworth to admit he had taken a gun into the store with him at the time it was robbed. Hileman then moved in for the kill.

HILEMAN: "Mr. Hollingsworth, you're guilty, aren't you?"
HOLLINGSWORTH: "No."
HILEMAN: "Mr. Hollingsworth, you're guilty, aren't you?"
HOLLINGSWORTH: "Yeah."

Prosecutor Hileman was stunned. "I couldn't believe it," he said. "I quit after that." When Hollingsworth's trial resumed the following day, the jury, because of his lack of a criminal record, or his amazing honesty, gave the convicted robber only five years in prison. They could have given him life.

It is against the law in Las Vegas, Nevada, to pawn your dentures.

A Rose by Any Other Name Would Still Smell as Sweet

The defense attorney for Tyrone Jerrols of Houston, Texas, who was facing charges of murder, filed a motion to prevent the use of Jerrols's nickname, claiming it would prejudice the jury. Jerrols's nickname is "Hitman."

According to Oklahoma common law, "Insanity is not evidenced when a widow, anxious to marry, shows her love letters from one suitor to another, and boasts constantly about her conquests, both real and those imagined."

Tackling Discrimination

In 1989 Francis Scott Key High School in Union Bridge, Maryland, was under pressure from a new federal statute which banned discrimination on the basis of gender. The school board members were afraid if they disallowed anyone from participating in sports because of sex they would be setting themselves up for a major lawsuit. That's how Tawana Hammond, 17, became the first female running back in the school's history. Unfortunately, she didn't make it past the first scrimmage. When she was tackled during the first play she fell on the knees of an opposing player, was hurt, and eventually suffered the loss of half her pancreas. In October 1992 Tawana filed a lawsuit against the Carroll County Board of Education for $1.5 million on the grounds that no one had explained to her "the potential risks of serious and disabling injury inherent in the sport." An example of unsportswomanlike conduct—or just someone who's never watched Monday night football? You make the call.

In Hot Springs, Arkansas, it is illegal to gargle in public.

A Jury of Your Peers

When Plymouth, Massachusetts, resident Anthony Varrasso received a letter calling him to report for jury duty, he couldn't believe they wanted him. Varrasso was short on experience in dealing with city hall and asked his mother, Lisa Varrasso, for her assistance. Mrs. Varrasso was informed by state officials that the last census form listed Anthony as being 18 years of age, and therefore he must report for duty or be held accountable. Anthony appeared at the Plymouth Superior Court on the date specified on his summons and looked up at the judge. The judge looked down at him and saw little three-year-old Anthony Varrasso nervously holding his mother Lisa's hand. Court officer Nanci Cordiero told Anthony, "You're Anthony? We'd love to have you here but you're a little too young." The other potential jurors broke out in a spontaneous round of applause for the junior jurist and Cordiero gave Anthony a tour of the court. Massachusetts has been plagued with faulty jury summonses in the past. Among some of the potential jurors selected at random by computer have been pets, dead people, and buildings. ➡

In Klamath Falls, Oregon, you are not allowed to kick the heads off snakes.

Take Pride in Your City —or Else!

"It is prohibited for pedestrians and motorists to display frowns, grimaces, scowls, threatening and glowering looks, gloomy and depressed facial appearances, generally all of which reflect unfavorably upon the city's reputation."
—*a Pocatello, Idaho, ordinance*

In Los Angeles, California, you are not allowed to hunt moths under a streetlight.

To Thine Own Self Be True

Peter Maxwell of Chino, California, is his own boss—literally. He and his wife own 95 percent of a urethane manufacturing company. Maxwell is also on the payroll as a worker, so Maxwell is both the owner and an employee. Maxwell, the boss, was pretty stingy, however and paid Maxwell, the employee, only $10,000 a year. One day while Maxwell, the employee, was operating a mixing machine, his sweater became entangled on an exposed bolt and he was pulled into the device, which severely injured him. Maxwell, the employee, hired an attorney and sued Maxwell, the owner, for negligence and sought damages for his injuries. Maxwell, the owner, hired another lawyer to defend the company against the lawsuit. Strangely enough, both Maxwells decided they could settle their dispute out of court and negotiated that Maxwell, the owner, should pay Maxwell, the employee, $122,500 for his injuries. When the IRS got wind of the deal it was not pleased. It demanded that Maxwell, the employee, pay $64,185 of the settlement in income tax. It also insisted that Maxwell, the owner, cough up $58,500 because he tried to write off the payment to Maxwell, the employee, as a business expense. Maxwell was outraged—and so was Maxwell. Maxwell, the owner, side by side with Maxwell, the employee, appealed the IRS's judgment to the U.S. Tax Court. In 1990 Judge Robert Ruwe ruled that Maxwell, the employee, could have the settlement income tax-free and that Maxwell, the owner, could deduct the $58,500 as a business expense.

Citizens of Garfield County, Montana, are not allowed to draw funny faces on their window shades.

Quick Convict Cases #1

Just in case you haven't had enough of those zany inmates and their wacky lawsuits—here's more!

- A New York inmate who claimed he was locked in his cell for taking an extra piece of cake in the mess hall was awarded $200 in damages.

- Indiana inmate, Mark Fast, who is serving 12 years for burglary, won his lawsuit against Mahlon Rieke, II, in December 1992. Rieke, whose house had just been robbed by Fast, shot Fast while he ran away. Fast sued on the grounds that the injury made sleeping and sitting down painful. He was awarded $12,250.

- Douglas Jackson, a Florida inmate, has filed dozens of lawsuits, including one because the prison served him cold food, and another because he was forced to watch "junk TV" since he didn't have access to public television.

In Washington, D.C., it's against the law to paint lemons on the side of your car in order to embarrass your car dealer.

The Outlaw Lawsuit Suit

Michael S. Allen appeared in court wearing the best outfit he had, an olive-green, double-breasted suit, because he wanted to make a good impression on the judge. Allen, then 26, along with an accomplice faced charges of credit card fraud, carrying a concealed weapon, and auto theft in Flint, Michigan. According to Mundy Township Detective Tom Hosie, the gun carried by Allen's alleged partner had been stolen from a Groveland Township home a few weeks earlier. The homeowner had been called to court to testify about the theft of the weapon and happened to see Allen standing outside the courtroom doors. The man walked up to Mundy Township Police Chief David Guigear and Hosie and asked if Allen was involved in the burglary case. The officers asked why the man wanted to know, and the man replied, "Because he's wearing my suit." The suit's custom-made label verified his claim. It was also discovered that, since the suit was a few sizes too large, Allen was wearing a sweat suit underneath the suit to make it fit correctly.

A law in Fruithill, Kentucky, demands that a man must remove his hat when coming face-to-face with a cow on any public road.

A Second Helping of O. J.

"If you see it on TV, switch to 'The Simpsons.' The TV show, I mean," warned Judge Lance Ito to the potential jurors in the O. J. Simpson trial. Everyone involved in the trial has been criticized for something, but no one took more heat than the jury. What do we know about the jurors? Check out the facts:

The jury was sequestered for *266* days.
Jurors reviewed *857* pieces of evidence.
More than *200* proceedings were held in its presence.
The jury listened to *126* witnesses . . .
and went through a total of *40,000* pages of evidence.
But it took the jury only *4* hours to reach a decision.

The Sixth Amendment to the Constitution refers to a "speedy and public trial"—is this what our forefathers had in mind?

In Hartford, Connecticut, it is illegal to walk across the street on your hands.

Bingo-o-o-o-o-o-o-o-oh!

Seventy-three-year-old Mary Verdev was happily playing bingo at the St. Florian Catholic Church in Milwaukee, Wisconsin, in 1990, when she got the surprise of her life. As she scanned her card for the number that had just been called, the 300-pound bingo board, which was used to keep track of the numbers, collapsed on her head. Verdev sued the St. Florian Catholic Church, and the case came before Judge Patrick J. Madden. In her lawsuit Verdev claimed she sustained $90,000 in medical injuries, suffering from uncontrollable "spontaneous orgasms," sometimes in "clusters," and found herself sexually attracted to women for the first time in her life. The attorney for St. Florian's, James Green, claimed Verdev suffered no more than a small bump on the head and a bruised arm. Judge Madden, of the Milwaukee circuit court, agreed with attorney Green when he argued, "It is unexplained in modern medicine how a bump on the head can alter sexual orientation or cause recurring orgasms." The judge ordered Verdev to undergo psychological examination. Verdev refused. It was a full six years later in April 1996, before the lawsuit was finally dismissed. On a personal note, at age 73, I don't know if the word "suffering" could be used to describe spontaneous orgasms.

In Kentucky it is illegal to fire a gun that isn't loaded.

Getting Teed Off

Jeannine Pelletier had played golf at the Fort Kent Golf Club in Maine about 20 times before having an accident there in the late 1980s. She teed off at the first hole at the little nine-hole golf course, and her ball landed about 14 yards from a set of old railroad tracks. She eyed the green and took a mighty swing at the ball, which shot out like a rocket, hit the railroad tracks, ricocheted back, and hit Pelletier directly on the nose. Pelletier sued the golf course for negligence, seeking $250,000 in damages, but the jury awarded Pelletier's poorly aimed "fore" with only $40,000. Harold J. Friedman, the Portland attorney, whose law firm represented the golf course, explained that a golfer who struck a tree or a rock could have suffered the same injury. "This case doesn't belong in the courts," Friedman said. "The plaintiff should have seen her golf pro to straighten out her swing." The award was appealed, but the Supreme Judicial Court of Maine agreed with the trial court and in July 1994, let Pelletier keep the $40,000 award. At the same time, however, it denied Pelletier's husband the damages he sought. Gerald Pelletier was suing for damages because Mrs. Pelletier's nose was so sore she wouldn't have sex with him. "On the evidence before it," the Supreme Judicial Court stated, "the jury properly could have concluded that as a result of the injuries sustained by his wife, Gerald suffered no loss of continuation of relationship with her." Looks like Jeannine landed in the green, and Gerald landed in the rough.

In Lexington, Kentucky, it is against the law to place an ice-cream cone in your back pocket.

Well Put

An open court gives a lot of people reason to open their mouths. Sometimes when their mouths are open wide enough—they stick their feet in them.

● "[They were] two kids who had nothing better to do. They don't have cable TV—what do you do?"
—*Defense lawyer Paul Fernadex, citing a possible reason, in a Paterson, New Jersey, court in March 1994, as to why his client, a 14-year-old boy, might have sexually assaulted an 11-year-old girl*

● "Had I not been born with breasts, I would not have been prosecuted. It's not for attention. It's for civil rights."
—*Angelina Carreras, who was convicted of disorderly conduct by a Harris County, Texas, jury in 1994, after she bared her breasts at Sylvan Beach in La Porte*

● "I'm sellin' dope / And I was gettin' paid / Too blind to see / How I was gettin' played."
—*Eric Clark, then 22, rapped a plea to the judge for a light sentence in December 1994. He received 23 years in prison.*

It is against the law in Norfolk, Virginia, to have sex while riding in a motorcycle sidecar.

Go Directly to Jail.
Do not Pass Go.
Do not Collect $200.

Jorge Rodriguez, then 22, stood before a municipal judge in Kenosha, Wisconsin, without knowing how to speak English and without legal counsel. He had been charged with driving under the influence after he smashed into a parked car. Even with all this against him, Rodriguez knew he had the upper hand. After the judge berated him for his behavior, Rodriguez reached into his pocket, pulled out a card, and handed it to the judge. The card read "Get Out Of Jail Free," and had been printed, and handed out in the last election by a candidate for sheriff. "Clearly the defendant had the impression it was legitimate and was going to play that trump card," said the assistant city attorney. The judge, on the other hand, wanted more money for the community chest. He fined Rodriguez $1,107 and suspended his driver's license. Rodriguez didn't realize the judge had a "monopoly" on his future driving career; now he'll have to hitch a ride on the Reading Railroad.

**It is illegal in Los Angeles, California, for infants
to dance in public halls.**

I Don't Think So

No matter what happens, the accused always has a good excuse. Here's what I mean . . .

• In May 1996 Jenny Lee Owens, 39, explained to a London, Ohio, court why her boyfriend was shot to death. "Something came into the room. It was not a person. It was like a color. Me and it, whatever it was, we both had the gun. Somehow it had passed into me. It was holding the gun; I was standing behind it." Together Jenny Lee Owens and "it" walked down the hall, aimed the gun, and shot Jenny's boyfriend in the back of the head. Too bad "it" never showed up in court.

• Januice Brown was found guilty by a Texas jury in the shooting death of her husband. Brown's defense was that she killed her husband to prevent aliens from torturing him forever.

**In Fort Madison, Iowa, the fire department is required
by law to practice fire-fighting techniques for
15 minutes before attending any fire.**

The Judge's Heart Was in the Right Place

In 1993 Bartolome Moya, then 36, was arrested in Philadelphia and held on allegedly ordering six murders and several bombings in New York. Moya was placed in jail while he awaited trial, but a judge took pity on him because Moya had a bad heart. The judge thought Moya's death was imminent and decided to dismiss all charges against him. Great break for Moya—and his luck kept getting better. Of the 6,000 people who were on the list for heart transplants in 1994, only 2,000 received one and Moya was one of the lucky 2,000. Prosecutors soon learned of Moya's February transplant and moved to have the murder charges reinstated in May 1994. Once again, Moya was placed in jail awaiting his trial, and once again a judge released him, this time on the condition that Moya wear a beeper/monitor. In July 1994 Moya skipped town and hasn't been heard from since. The only way Moya will turn himself in is if he gets another change of heart.

South Dakota has decreed it illegal to fall asleep in a cheese factory.

Give Me Some Space

Eleanor Mellick, a retired schoolteacher in Chicago, was given the squeeze by her condo association in May 1993. The association narrowed Mellick's parking space from 111 inches to 93 inches to accommodate a new parking space for the board president. Eighteen inches is a lot of land in Chicago and Mellick complained to the association board about their unilateral decision. The board was deaf to Mellick's arguments and did nothing to resolve the matter, so Mellick sued. She filed suit against the board president, three board members, and the association, in November 1994. It took a year and eight months before Judge Thomas P. Durkin of the Cook County Circuit Court ruled on Mellick's complaint. In August 1996 the judge ruled against the board and its actions, stating: "[T]he plaintiff's version of the events is extremely credible, [while] the testimony of the defendants was cavalier and self-serving." The judge stopped the board from cutting into Mellick's space and ordered it to pay her $51,006 in damages, as well as her legal fees of $166,171. Looks like Mellick made the president of the board–walk while she kept her park-place.

**You are not allowed to wear patent leather shoes
in Oxford, Ohio.**

If You've Got It, Don't Flaunt It!

In Kentucky, "No female shall appear in a bathing suit on any highway within this state unless she be escorted by at least two officers or unless she be armed with a club." However, this Kentucky law goes on to say, "The provisions of this statute shall not apply to females weighing less than 90 pounds nor exceeding 200 pounds nor shall it apply to female horses."

In San Francisco, California, it is against the law to wet laundered clothing with water sprayed out of your mouth.

Legal Briefs

- In 1995 a Decatur, Georgia, judge returned a 14-year-old girl to the custody of her mother, even though the mother had tried to keep the girl from running away by chaining her ankles together.

- A federal judge granted protection to the jingle of Anabell's Ice Cream trucks in Glocester, Rhode Island, citing the First Amendment.

- In James McDougal's 1996 Whitewater trial, Barbara Adams was named an alternate juror. Adams, who likes to be referred to as "Commander," came to the courthouse attired in a red "Star Trek: The Next Generation" uniform, wearing a "phaser" and "tricorder" on her belt. "I stand for Star Trek ideals," said Adams. "Faith in your fellow man, avoiding war, peaceful resolution to adversaries, and avoiding prejudice."

- A child-rape case in Columbus, Ohio, was dismissed by the judge because a witness arrived 20 minutes late. Prosecutors have announced they will not appeal the ruling.

- In 1995 Life Management, a Salt Lake City, Utah, company dedicated to self-esteem, sued the Mormon Church for $189 million over the church's policy of encouraging members to exclusively use the Bible to seek guidance.

- A prosecutor in Kenton County, Kentucky, threw a woman in jail because her son owed a $3 library fine.

It is forbidden in Miami, Florida, to imitate animals.

All the News That's Fit to Print

In 1990 the supermarket tabloid, the *Sun,* ran a headline that read "World's Oldest Newspaper Carrier, 101, Quits Because She's Pregnant." The story told of a newspaper carrier in Stirling, Australia, named Audrey Wills, who was forced to resign her position because her affair with a millionaire on her route had left her pregnant. The article ran with an accompanying photograph of the sexually active senior citizen. The story was a hoax—there isn't even a town called Stirling in Australia—but the photograph was real. It was a picture of Nellie Mitchell, who owned a newspaper stand and who delivered the *Arkansas Gazette* until she was 90. Mitchell wasn't 101—she was 96 and still very much alive. Mitchell sued the *Sun* for $1 million, claiming the article and photograph were an invasion of privacy and had caused her "extreme emotional distress" because people pestered her with questions about when her baby was due. During the trial the editor of the *Sun,* John Vader, admitted he had selected the photograph because he had assumed Mitchell was dead. In her testimony Mitchell said she hadn't given birth within the last 61 years and that she'd never engaged in sexual activity with anyone on her paper route. The Arkansas jury sided with Mitchell and awarded her $1.5 million, which was later reduced by a judge to $1 million. Read all about it!

It is illegal for any driver of an automobile to be blindfolded while operating the vehicle in Birmingham, Alabama.

How Do You Spell Relief?

The competition was fierce. There were only two finalists left. One of them would be the winner and go on to compete again—the other would go home. Thirteen-year-old Steven Chen and 12-year-old Victor Wang were duking it out to determine who would represent Los Altos School in the 1987 Ventura County, California, Spelling Bee. The word was drawn and Victor approached the microphone. H-O-R-S-Y. Correct! Now it was Steven's turn. H-O-R-S-E-Y. Sorry, that's incorrect! Contest officials disqualified Steven and advanced Victor to the county finals. Steven knew something was wrong, and went home to check his trusty dictionary; sure enough, both spellings of "horsy" were in the dictionary. The contest officials decided it would only be fair if both boys attended the county finals.

It was at the finals that 13-year-old defending champion, Gavin McDonald, was defeated by Steven Chen. Steven then advanced to the national spelling bee. Gavin's father nearly had a spell and decided to file a $2 million lawsuit against the *Ventura County Star-Free Press,* the county event's sponsor, charging mental distress. The complaint claimed that Steven Chen should not have been allowed to compete because the rules stated that each school was allowed only one entrant. The lawsuit was dismissed by both a superior court judge and the state court of appeals. As for the judgment of the trial court, "appellate Judge Arthur Gilbert ruled, 'We'll spell it out: A-F-F-I-R-M-E-D.'" The judges ruled that Gavin McDonald lost the Ventura County spelling bee not because Steven Chen was allowed to participate, or whether or not the contest had been poorly run, but because he failed to properly spell the word "iridescent." ➡

In Tylertown, Mississippi, it is against the law for any man to shave in the middle of Main Street.

Don't Judge a Crook by His Cover

The attorney for Christopher Plovie, who was on trial for drug possession in 1990, claimed his client had been illegally searched because the officer didn't have a warrant. In countering that claim, the prosecution stated the officer didn't need a warrant because a "bulge" in Plovie's jacket, which could have been a gun, gave the officer probable cause to search. Plovie, who was wearing the same jacket in the Pontiac, Michigan, court that day, was outraged. He handed the jacket to the judge to prove that the material the jacket was made of simply didn't bulge. Upon examining the jacket, the judge reached into one of the pockets and pulled out a packet of cocaine.

In Altoona, Pennsylvania, it is against the law for a baby-sitter to raid her employer's refrigerator.

A Carbonated Romeo and Juliet

In 1985 Amanda Blake of Northampton, Massachusetts, who had been a loyal employee of the Coca-Cola Bottling Company for eight years, fell in love with, and become engaged to, David Cronin, who worked for Coca-Cola's arch rival, Pepsi. Coke demanded that Blake, a data processing manager at the Coca-Cola Bottling Company, either break off her engagement, persuade Cronin to leave Pepsi, or resign from her position at Coca-Cola. Blake nearly popped her top when she was given these options and decided not to do anything of the sort. Coca-Cola promptly fired her for "conflict of interest." "I was more sad than mad after all the hours and time I put in," said Blake, "and then they didn't think twice about firing me." But Blake spun the bottle on Coca-Cola and sued for damages, winning a $600,000 settlement. Now that's the real thing!

In Rayville, Maryland, it is against the law for fishermen to read comic books while fishing on a lake or river.

The Prison Files Part 2

Since prisoners can escape neither the boredom of their surroundings, nor the confines of their cells, they escape to prison law libraries for occasionally frivolous escapades. (Over 15 percent of all federal civil suits are filed by prisoners.)

● Several Minnesota inmates have filed lawsuits claiming "cruel and unusual punishment" because they were provided with an improper variety of beans on their menu.

● Robert Lee Brock, an inmate at the Indian Creek Correction Center in Chesapeake, Virginia, filed a $5 million lawsuit against Robert Lee Brock. Brock claimed that Brock, himself, violated his religious beliefs and his civil rights by forcing himself to get himself drunk—and because of this self-induced drunkenness he perpetrated several crimes. Brock, who is serving 23 years for breaking and entering and grand larceny, wrote, "I partook of alcoholic beverages in 1993, July 1, as a result I caused myself to violate my religious beliefs. This was done by my going out and getting arrested." He went on to claim, "I want to pay myself $5 million [for violating my own rights] but ask the state to pay it in my behalf since I can't work and am a ward of the state." Judge Rebecca Beach Smith dismissed the claim in April 1995.

● Three inmates in Idaho filed a $10.7 million lawsuit claiming "cruel and unusual punishment" because guards failed to give them late-night snacks.

"A one-armed piano player may be seen, but not if admission is charged to view his performance."
—an Iowa law

Turning Zzzzzz's into $$$$$$$$$$

A 31-year-old woman from Northern California sued city hall, after she was hauled into court for snoring too loudly. The woman shared a common wall with a neighbor, and when her snoring kept him awake, the neighbor called the police. A California Noise Enforcement Officer issued the woman a $50 citation in 1994 at 1:30 AM. The citation was eventually dismissed, but then the woman filed a lawsuit seeking damages of $24,000 for stress, lost wages, and other losses (loss of sleep wasn't mentioned). "Periodically, I go to new places and get recognized and that's very uncomfortable for me," said the plaintiff. "I feel like crawling under the sofa or something." The lawsuit was finally settled for $13,500 in March 1995. "I'm happy that we settled out of court," the woman said. "But as far as this being truly over, it will never be truly over until the city stops doing stupid things." I wouldn't lose any sleep over it.

It is a violation of Vermont state law to whistle while underwater.

A Pointed Law

"Any person who shall wear in a public place any device or thing attached to her head, hair, headgear or hat, which device or thing is capable of lacerating the flesh of any other person with whom it may come in contact and which is not sufficiently guarded against the possibility of so doing, shall be adjudged a disorderly person."
—*a Secaucus, New Jersey, ordinance*

It is against the law in Idaho to fish for trout while sitting on the back of a giraffe.

Well Put as Well

- "Fifty dollars for what? I got life without parole, and I got to pay $50?"
—*Eddie Robertson, Jr., after being sentenced to life without parole by a Tuscaloosa, Alabama, judge who also imposed a $50 fine payable to a victim-compensation fund*

- "I am kind of glad the kids are gone. Now I can go out and do what I want. It's all about freedom."
—*Shervonne Pryor made that statement to a detective after murdering her two-year-old daughter, Lakeesha. Even though Pryor admitted she had placed a pillow over the girl's face, the judge cleared her, concluding that the medical examiner probably wouldn't have listed Lakeesha's death as a homicide had Pryor not confessed. Pryor's three other children had already been placed in foster homes.*

- "God ordained the killing of animals. He himself killed animals to provide skins for Adam and Eve after they sinned."
—*District Judge Warren Litynski of St. Peter, Minnesota, in 1991, explaining why he fined a man only $1 for leaving five puppies to suffocate to death in a trash bin*

It is against the law in Tennessee to drive a car while you are asleep.

Skirting the Law

During his January 1993 trial for murdering his wife, defendant Robert J. Kosilek of New Bedford, Massachusetts, asked if he could alter the court's dress code. Kosilek, who also insisted on being called Michelle, received permission to wear women's clothing during the proceedings: slacks, an angora sweater, and makeup. The Bristol County Assistant District Attorney, John Moses, said, "I don't think it had any real impact on the jury one way or another." After cross-examining the cross-dresser, Moses stated, "The issue was not whether he was a woman trapped in a man's body, but whether he was responsible for his conduct." He was. Robert J. Kosilek was found guilty of the murder of his wife on January 25, 1993. Kosilek's motive behind killing his wife was never made clear—I wonder if he wanted her wardrobe.

Wisconsin law states that apple pie cannot be served or eaten anywhere in the state without a slice of cheese on top.

Too Close for Comfort

Joseph Green Brown and his partner, Ronald Floyd, committed a robbery in Florida. Brown felt remorseful and turned himself in. He confessed to the robbery and told police that Floyd had been his partner. So the police arrested Floyd, who was understandably pissed off at being ratted out. In retaliation Floyd told the police about a murder that Brown had confessed to him. At the murder trial, Brown tried to explain to the judge and jury that Floyd was making up the story of the murder confession because he was angry at him. Brown also explained that Floyd was getting a deal from the D.A. for the bogus incrimination. Brown was convicted of first-degree murder in 1974 and sentenced to death. Two months after the conviction, Floyd said that he had been lying and that Brown didn't do anything. (He later retracted his retraction when threatened with a perjury charge, but later said again that the original testimony he had given was a lie.) Brown spent nearly 14 years on death row waiting for the day that would be his last. He exhausted his appeal; the state supreme court agreed with the lower court's ruling, and the execution was going to take place. Just 13 hours before Brown was scheduled to die, the Eleventh Circuit Court of Appeals granted him a new trial, saying, "The prosecution knowingly allowed material false testimony to be introduced at trial." In March 1987, a year after the court of appeals ruling, the state decided not to retry the case, and Brown was released.

It is illegal to slap a man on the back in Georgia.

A Cliché Come to Life

In January 1996 Stewart Marshall was found guilty of assaulting his wife. After announcing the verdict, Judge Joel Gehrke called Marshall to the bench and ordered him to hold out his hand. Marshall did as he was told, and Judge Gehrke gave him a light three-fingered slap on the wrist and admonished him by saying, "Don't do that!" This action started a whirlwind of public outrage against the judge. But Gehrke felt a simple "slap on the wrist" punishment was justified, since Marshall's wife had become pregnant by Marshall's brother and recently given birth to Marshall's nephew.

"No person shall disturb the occupant of any house by knocking on the door or ringing the bell. Nor shall a person yell, stomp, pound on, or kick a door to get the attention of the occupant or occupants."
—*a Bridgewater, New Jersey, ordinance*

Treated Like a King

When the lawyers who formed Rodney King's legal defense, all 23 of them, submitted their legal bill to the city of Los Angeles, California, it was a real whack on the side of the head. They demanded $4.4 million in legal fees for 13,000 hours of work, at fees ranging up to $350 an hour. Most of the time was spent preparing for court, but some of the hours billed were for lawyers' time on talk shows, taking King to movie and theater premieres, attending his birthday party, and prompting him for the news conference during which he made the spontaneous plea of, "Can't we all get along?" King's settlement was for $3.8 million, so his lawyers were asking $600,000 more than King. One of the last items billed was time spent in countering negative publicity after King was arrested the second time for attempting to evade police. During the evasion, King nearly ran down a police officer before he was finally caught. He was in the company of a transvestite prostitute at the time. "All I'm asking for is a day's wage for a day's work," said one of King's lawyers, Steven A. Lerman. Evidently the lawyers aren't going to take a beating, either.

In Macomb, Illinois, it is against the law for an automobile to impersonate a wolf.

Poor Judgment

In January 1996 a 41-year-old ex-pastor from Florida pleaded guilty to persuading his six-year-old daughter to touch him in a sexual manner while he videotaped her. There was an outpouring of support from the community for their former pastor, so the judge repealed the normal three-year prison term and instead sentenced him to house arrest. Sound fair? The ex-pastor was sentenced to serve his time in the house he still shared with his daughter.

In Los Angeles, California, it is legal for a man to beat his wife with a strap or leather belt. However, the husband may not strike his wife with a belt wider than two inches unless he has his wife's permission.

Justice in the End

Convicted murderer Michael Anderson Godwin, then 28, was originally sentenced to the electric chair but, after years of appeals, got his sentence reduced to life in prison. In 1983 at the Central Correctional Institution in Columbia, South Carolina, Godwin attempted to fix a pair of earphones connected to his television set. While sitting on the steel toilet in his cell, Godwin stripped the earphone wire with his teeth and electrocuted himself.

"No young woman shall sit on a man's lap without a cushion or a pillow under her."
—a Lawton, Oklahoma, ordinance

The Law Offices of Dewy, Cheatum, and Howe

In 1993 relatives of two of the Three Stooges, Curly-Joe DeRita's widow and Larry Fine's granddaughter, sued the estate of founding Stooge, Moe Howard. DeRita's widow and Fine's granddaughter filed a suit against Norman Maurer Productions (Norman is Moe's son-in-law), Moe's daughter Joan, and grandson Jeffry Scott, claiming they were owed about $5 million in profits from film rights and various Stooge merchandise. The unequal distribution of wealth made Jean DeRita eye-gouging mad. "I know that Moe would not approve of this," said the widow of the last of the Stooges, Curly-Joe, shortly before he died in 1993. "He always said that he got what Larry got, what Curly-Joe got. Moe would turn over in his grave if he knew what they were doing." Looks like Moe was busy rolling over because in July 1994 Jean DeRita and Larry's grandchildren once again filed a lawsuit against the estate of Moe Howard seeking $1 million in damages. This time they claimed Las Vegas-based MGM Grand Hotel and theme park profited from using the trio's names, faces, voices, and routines and signed a exclusive licensing agreement with only Moe's survivors. But in December 1994, Moe's relatives took a legal pie-in-the-face when a Los Angeles jury awarded Jean DeRita and Larry Fine's grandchildren over $2 million. Ain't that a poke in the eye! Nyuk, nyuk, nyuk.

In Portland, Maine, it is against the law to tickle a girl under the chin with a feather duster.

Judgment Daze #1

Some judges show great leniency in sentencing; others throw the book at guilty parties (and then some).

• Frustrated by the routine release of women convicted of misdemeanor prostitution, one judge in San Francisco set a hooker's bail at $5 billion.

• Gilbert Franklin Rhodes, convicted of first-degree murder, was sentenced to serve the rest of his natural life in New Mexico's Department of Corrections—followed by two years' parole.

• In 1981 Deuel Wilhelm Davies of Tuscaloosa, Alabama, was sentenced to 10,000 years in prison for a triple murder, one of his victims being his mother-in-law. ➡

"No one shall drive any kind of motorized vehicle while said vehicle is running while dipping snuff or chewing tobacco."
—a McAlester, Oklahoma, ordinance

Well, Shut My Mouth

In 1993 Federal Judge Joyce Hens Green ruled that the Washington, D.C., fire department had violated the civil rights of one of its firefighters when it had prohibited him from performing mouth-to-mouth resuscitation. The judge overruled the fire department's ban, even though the firefighter had hepatitis B, which is 100 times more contagious than AIDS and kills nearly 7,000 people a year.

Cats are forbidden to ride on a public bus in Seattle, Washington, if there is a dog already on board. Also any dog weighing greater than 25 pounds must pay the full adult fare.

School Daze

A terrible tragedy occurred in 1995 when a nine-year-old girl was raped by a 12-year-old boy, both of whom attended a special-education class at Gregory School on Chicago, Illinois's, West Side. The girl's parents filed a lawsuit against the school, citing negligence on the part of the school to prevent such an occurrence. In response, the board of education blamed not the boy, not the school, but the little nine-year-old victim because she had failed to cry adequately for help. "Any injuries sustained occurred by [the] plaintiff's negligent failure to exercise ordinary care." I thought special-education classes were to help slower-thinking children—not hinder them by slower-thinking adults.

It is against the law in Chicago, Illinois, to hug your neighbor against her wishes.

Quick Convict Cases #2

• A Utah prisoner filed a $1 million lawsuit against the state for suspending a program which provided hair transplants for prisoners. He claimed "emotional suffering."

• Reginald Troy, an inmate with ulcers in New York's Shawangunk Correctional Facility in Wallkill, sued the prison claiming "violation of constitutional rights" because he was not provided lamb, veal, and oysters for his meals. These foods are approved, but not prescribed by his doctor.

• Roy Clendinen, a prisoner at the Mohawk Correctional Facility near Syracuse, New York, sued for $1 million because a guard wouldn't put his ice cream in the freezer and it had melted.

• Inmates at the county jail in Salem, Massachusetts, sued the Essex County sheriff and other officials for "cruel and unusual conditions," citing among other charges, multiple bunking and the fact that they had no way to exercise during the winter. They were awarded $2 million, with 12 percent interest from the time the case was settled until the time they collected their winnings.

By law, morticians in Shreveport, Louisiana, may not advertise their services by printing the names of their funeral parlors on pencils.

Pay No Attention to the Man Inside Your Head

The State of New Jersey was named in a $14 million lawsuit filed by Ned Searight in 1976 claiming he had suffered injuries while in custody in 1962. Searight charged that while he was a ward of the state, he was unlawfully and against his will, injected with a "radium electric beam." As a result of the injection, Searight claimed a voice spoke to him from inside his head. The United States District Court dismissed the claim, not on the grounds that it was frivolous, but because the statute of limitations had run out—Searight had filed his claim too late. The judge wrote in his opinion, "But taking the facts as pleaded . . . they show a case of presumably unlicensed radio communication, a matter which comes within the sole jurisdiction of the Federal Communications Commission. . . . And even aside from that, Searight could have blocked the broadcast to the antenna in his brain simply by grounding it. . . . Searight might have pinned to the back of a trouser leg a short chain of paper clips so that the end would touch the ground and prevent anyone from talking to him inside his brain." A finally tuned opinion, don't you think?

You are not allowed to drag a rope through any street in Cumberland, Maryland.

The More the Merrier

In 1988 Frederick E. Mayhue was found guilty in an Allegheny County, Pennsylvania, court of beating, strangling, and finally shooting to death his wife, Harlene, from whom he had been separated for five years. But in 1994 the Pennsylvania Supreme Court changed Mayhue's sentence from "death" to "life in prison." During the course of the lower court trial, it came to light that Mayhue, on at least three separate occasions, had hired someone else to kill his wife. The supreme court ruled that the jury was incorrect in considering Mayhue's nearly four-year crusade to have his wife killed as an "aggravating circumstance" before handing down the death sentence. "None of the three contracts to kill caused any harm whatsoever to the victim," Justice Frank J. Montemuro wrote. "All of their agreements had clearly been breached and abandoned months before Mrs. Mayhue was murdered. Rather, the sole cause of this brutal crime was appellant's intent to kill his wife."

Harlene Mayhue was found dead in the trunk of her car in December 1986 shortly after leaving her daughter's birthday party. She had been pummeled with a baseball bat, strangled, and shot between the eyes. Frederick Mayhue confessed that he involved nearly ten people in the murder scheme before he finally did it himself. Because, if you want something done right . . .

"Any services performed by a jackass must be recorded."
—*a Baltimore, Maryland, law*

A Dash of Justice

In December 1993 Dennis Scheib, an attorney practicing in Atlanta, Georgia, briefly stopped by the Fulton County solicitor's office on his way to the State Court Building to meet his newest client. As he was leaving the office, Scheib noticed two police officers in hot pursuit of a man who was running down the hall. The officers yelled out that the man had escaped them, and ordered him to stop. Scheib dropped his briefcase and ran with the two officers to help recapture the man. The police officers slapped the handcuffs on the escapee and took him away. "I just caught a glimpse of him and I thought he looked familiar, but nothing really clicked," said Scheib. "It wasn't until I got in the courtroom that it dawned on me that I had just helped capture my own client."

In Decatur, Illinois, it is against the law to drive a car without a steering gear.

Foot in Mouth Defense

"A person who represents himself in court has a fool for a client," or so the saying goes. You be the judge.

● "I should have blown your f . . . king head off! If I'd been the one that was there."
—*Dennis Newton, in an Oklahoma City courtroom in 1985, reacting to a witness who identified him as the person who held up a gas station*

● "You guys are so unfair!"
—*Donita Jo Artis, then 24, to the judge and prosecutors in a Pittsburgh, Pennsylvania, court. Artis was denied custody of her three-year-old son after she beat him until he was blind, deaf, and unable to walk.*

● "One of the main regrets that I have is that I wasn't able to take the chain saw to the rest of my family."
—*Kevin Rocrod, then 28, at his sentencing in November 1994 when asked by the judge if he had any regrets about killing his father with a chain saw*

**Los Angeles, California, makes it illegal to use the U.S.
Postal Service to complain about cockroaches
in your hotel room.**

A Slice of Life

In March 1995 Jerry Williams, considered a habitual criminal under California's "three-strikes" law, was sentenced to 25 years to life. What was the crime that put Williams away for good? He stole a slice of pizza from a group of children on a Redondo Beach pier. Justice is served.

It is against the law in Ola, South Dakota, for any person to lay down in the middle of the road and take a nap. It is also against the law to do the same thing in Anniston, Oklahoma.

On Second Thought . . .

Robert Clinton Robinette, who was up on prostitution and child-sex charges in June 1994, decided to turn down a plea bargain of four years in prison offered by the district attorney in Gainesville, Florida. Robinette, believing he could get a better offer, fired the lawyer who suggested he take the deal and paid a $50,000 retainer to hire a new attorney. The new attorney set about renegotiating a plea bargain for Robinette on the same charges, and in April 1995 the best deal he could manage was a ten-year prison sentence. Not wanting to push his luck a third time, Robinette accepted.

**A Connecticut law makes it illegal to
"entice the bees of a neighbor."**

Not Helpless Enough

In the late 1980s, Lee Curtis Davis raped a 13-year-old girl with muscular dystrophy in Bartow, Florida. During his trial in 1987, Davis was convicted of sexual battery of a physically helpless person and sentenced to life in prison. Sexual battery is Florida's legal term for rape. But in 1991 the Second District Court of Appeals decided that Davis had been prosecuted under the wrong charge. Someone who is "physically helpless" is defined in the Florida statute as someone "asleep, unconscious or physically unable to communicate unwillingness." Even though the 13-year-old girl had muscular dystrophy, the appeals court decided she couldn't be considered helpless because she had screamed for help and tried to push Davis away. The Second District Court of Appeals changed Davis's original conviction from sexual battery of a physically helpless person to two counts of misdemeanor battery and sentenced him to one year in jail. Davis was given credit for time served and immediately released. A clear case of a physically challenged girl versus a mentally challenged court.

It is illegal in Trenton, New Jersey, to throw a tainted pickle into the street.

A Dead Beat Tenant

In early 1996 a California judge ruled against James Pflugradt's estate and in favor of Pflugradt's former landlord. The judge said the landlord could keep Pflugradt's $825 security deposit because Pflugradt died without giving 30 days' notice.

"Any person who shall not lift his hat to the Mayor as he passes him on the street will be guilty of a misdemeanor."
—*a Columbus, Montana, ordinance*

Warren Burger—or Twitty Burger?

Judges take a great deal of license when they render a judgment—some of them even take poetic license. In *Jenkins v. Commissioner,* Harold Jenkins, known to country music fans as Conway Twitty, hit a sour note in his dealings with the IRS. Conway, with other investors, started a business called Twitty Burger which eventually failed. Instead of everyone getting burned by this bad burger business, Conway, out of his own pocket, slowly paid off each and every investor. He then wanted to take his payments as a tax deduction. The IRS thought otherwise.

U.S. Tax Court Judge Leo H. Irwin, obviously inspired by the singer-songwriter, gave his opinion of the case in a poem he called "Ode to Conway Twitty."

> *Twitty Burger went belly up*
> *But Conway remained true,*
> *He repaid his investors, one and all,*
> *It was the moral thing to do.*
> *His fans would not have liked it,*
> *It could have hurt his fame*
> *Had any investors sued him*
> *Like Merle Haggard or Sonny James.*
> *When it was time to file taxes*
> *Conway thought what he would do*
> *Was deduct those payments as a business expense*
> *Under section one-sixty-two.*
> *In order to allow these deductions,*
> *Goes the argument of the Commissioner,*
> *The payments must be ordinary and necessary*
> *To a business of the petitioner.*

Had Conway not repaid the investors
His career would have been under cloud,
Under the unique facts of this case
Held: The deductions are allowed.

The IRS responded rhythmically:

Business, the court held,
It's deductible they feel;
We disagree with the answer
But let us not appeal.

In New York, pickles cannot be sold as a side dish in restaurants. They must "accompany a meal as a substitute for butter."

The Tail End of the Law

A street artist who worked in the West End of Dallas, Texas, peddled a pretty exclusive style of art—or so he thought. Krandel Lee Newton's specialty was drawing people's buttocks. He was the bottom line in butt sketching and even trademarked his business "Butt Sketch." But in 1992 another street artist, Mark Burton, rear-ended Newton's line of artistic expression and also began drawing pictures of people's bottoms. Burton gave his business the name "Fanny Sketch." Newton wasn't going to turn the other cheek on this intrusion into his livelihood; he filed a federal lawsuit accusing Burton of threatening his business. Burton soon realized he could get his butt kicked in federal court and decided to settle with Newton. Burton promised to stop using the name Fanny Sketch and to discontinue doing posterior portraits which might cause people to confuse his work with Mr. Newton's. I'm sure if Newton had taken Burton to trial, a good lawyer would have found a crack in the case.

It is against the law in Tennessee to throw a banana peel on the sidewalk.

Legal History

In ancient Rome, long before the advent of the Christian Bible, Romans would swear to "tell the truth, the whole truth, and nothing but the truth" by placing their right hand on their testicles. It is from this ritual that we derived the term "testimony." I wonder what happened when a woman was called to the witness stand.

"No male person shall make remarks to or concerning, or cough or whistle at, or do anything to attract the attention of any woman upon traveling along any of the sidewalks."
—*an Abilene, Texas, law*

Passing the Bar

During a 1989 divorce hearing, Judge Paul M. Marko, III, of Broward County, Florida, told Marianne Price, then 33, that he forbade her from having male suitors visit her or stay the night in her house because it was formerly joint property. The judge further stated that since Price's husband was now staying in his "own" apartment he could have the "entire [Miami] Dolphins cheerleading squad running though his apartment naked." Judge Marko then suggested to Price that she start frequenting singles bars: "I've been [in singles bars]. I'm a single man. There are all kinds of . . . guys running around in open shirts with eagles on their chests. There are great guys out there." The judge then explained to Price that if she was caught having a live-in lover, he would order her house to be sold, saying, "I don't want her all of a sudden taking up with some nice, sweet, little blond from Norway." Later Judge Marko apologized, saying, "I was wrong. I said it. It wasn't what I intended to say, but they are the words I used." The judge's decision was overturned by a higher court and he received a public reprimand in 1992.

In Louisville, Kentucky, it is against the law for a business owner to install an air-conditioning system which blows air through sidewalk grates and could potentially lift a woman's skirt.

A Judicial Shoe-in

When Robert Litchfield, a Nevada County, California, candidate for superior court judge in April 1996, received early poll results, he saw his name near the bottom of the list. As a gesture of his desire to serve and to gain a little publicity, Litchfield asked Nevada County's 170-plus attorneys to attend a local bar association meeting in early May so he could—wash their feet. "It is intended to be a gesture of humbling, of apology, if necessary, and of healing," he wrote in his April letter. Litchfield arrived at the event complete with basin and towel ready to scrub some soles, but there were no takers. A number of lawyers showed up at the function, mainly to show their support, but nary a loafer, pump, sneaker or flat was removed. Reacting to the media's inquiry of the foot-washing function, Litchfield said, "What I [offered] was an act of faith, and I don't think that's something a news reporter can understand."

"Shoes are required to eat in any restaurant or other place serving food to the public."
—*a strangely phrased law from Redding, California*

Guilty Before Proven Innocent

The courthouse was crowded in Waterbury, Connecticut, with 67 prospective jurors from whom the final jury would be selected for a triple-murder case. Superior Court Judge Maxwell J. Heinman was perched on his bench watching the mundane and time-consuming roll call of the jurors present. After each name was called, the juror would answer "Here," as they had been instructed. But when the court clerk called out the name Richard C. Dobbins, Jr., Mr. Dobbins raised his hand and yelled, "Guilty!" The judge fined Mr. Dobbins $100 and was forced to disqualify the 66 other jurors because of the judgmental slip-of-the-lip.

"Motorists may not back their automobiles into trees in public places."
—a Princeton, New Jersey, ordinance

Watching the Dominos Fall

"Thirty minutes or less or your pizza is free" used to be the battle cry of Dominos Pizza's delivery force. Now the battle cry is, "It'll get there when it gets there." Why? Because of a personal injury lawsuit filed against Dominos in late 1993. A woman in St. Louis, Missouri, suffered head and spinal cord injuries when a Domino's delivery van sped through a red light and smashed into her car. After a two-week trial, the jury awarded the woman $750,000 in actual damages and *$78 million* in punitive damages. The extremely high punitive award was probably imposed to stop negligent driving by delivery people trying to beat the half-hour deadline. Domino's management took the jury's order seriously and promptly discontinued their pizza policy—in 30 minutes or less.

"Bathing in the state of nudity in the water within the corporate limits of this Village" states a Spring Valley, New York, law, is forbidden between the hours of 5 AM and 8:30 PM.

And the Award Goes to . . .

People sue for a variety of reasons—usually for money. Depending on the skill of their attorney and the sympathy and gullibility of the jury, the award can really add up.

- A New York jury awarded $54 million in an asbestos case, which gave each of the three victims $18 million. How did they reach this settlement? The number "18" symbolizes "life" in Hebrew.

- A woman in New Mexico was awarded $2.9 million because the coffee she purchased at McDonald's burned her leg when the cup tipped over. A judge reduced the award to a mere $490,000 to deter bad "corporate coffee policy."

- A Harlingen, Texas, jury awarded a man $1.8 million in damages because he injured his knee when a small dog ran in front of his bicycle.

- A 45-year-old social worker left a Washington hospital with a scheduled tubal ligation, but with an unscheduled metal implement left in her body. The six-inch sheath caused her a year's worth of pain, but no permanent injury except a scar. The woman said she would settle for $400,000; the hospital said it would pay only $300,000. At the end of the trial the jury decided her pain and suffering was worth a little more—it awarded her $10 million. When asked how the jury had reached such an amount, one juror said, "Quite honestly, I think it had something to do with sounding like a round figure. . . . We were given no guidelines."

In Alaska it is against the law to look at a moose while riding in an airplane.

The Gamble That Didn't Pay Off

Toshi Van Blitter decided to take the biggest gamble of her life and sue Harrah's casinos in Las Vegas, Nevada. Van Blitter, of El Macero, California, played blackjack at two of the casinos and racked up $350,000 in debt. Since she hadn't done well at cards, she tried her hand at another suit—a lawsuit. In 1985 Van Blitter filed to have her debts canceled, claiming that Harrah's was negligent. For what? Van Blitter claimed Harrah's should have told her that she was an incompetent blackjack player or informed her that she should take classes on how to play the game. Her case went bust, however, when two federal judges dismissed her claim.

It is illegal in Xenia, Ohio, to spit in a salad bar.

The Suspense Is Killing Me

Donald Eugene Murray, then 52, watched fearfully as the jury left the box and went into the deliberation room to decide his fate. Murray was charged with sexual assault and on trial in August 1992 in a Gastonia, North Carolina, courtroom. Expecting the worst, he broke free and fled the courtroom. Moments later the jury came back to the courtroom with an empty defendant's chair and a verdict of "not guilty." An arrest warrant was issued for Murray's escape.

Residents of Kentucky are required by law to take a bath once a year.

An Unconventional Oven

Stanley E. Protokowicz of Maryland pled guilty in 1991 to breaking and entering the home of Nancy A. Sanders. Protokowicz, along with Sanders's estranged husband, Thomas Sanders, broke into the home during a drinking binge, received a 15-month suspended jail sentence and 18 months probation, and was sentenced to 40 hours of community service, fined $1,500, and made to pay the costs of psychiatric counseling for the young Sanders children. Protokowicz admitted that he placed the children's seven-month-old tabby kitten, Max, in the microwave but explained, "I didn't intend to hurt him. I was afraid he would get hurt with us moving around in the dark, so I put him in the microwave," Protokowicz said. "He was only in there for about five seconds. When we pulled him out, he was alive, but he didn't look too good." Once the intruders realized they had cooked the kitten, the two scaredy-cats left the house. The Sanders children were the first ones home after the incident and were severely traumatized upon finding their cooked pet. Protokowicz says he accidentally turned on the oven while searching for a switch for the overhead light. Nancy Sanders filed a disciplinary complaint with Maryland bar officials, claiming that despite what Protokowicz said, turning on the microwave is a four-step process which requires entering time, temperature, and other controls. In case you're wondering why Sanders contacted the Maryland bar officials, it's because Protokowicz is a practicing attorney. I guess that let the cat out of the bag.

In Massachusetts it is illegal for a goat to wear trousers.

You Said You Wanted the Truth

A young woman's mutilated body had been found near some railroad tracks, and David Huffman was the prime suspect. On the stand in a California courtroom, defendant David Huffman, then 20, was testifying to his whereabouts on the night of the murder. Huffman had already confessed that he and a friend had engaged in sex with the woman, then had decided not to pay her even though they had had a deal. But then he decided to elaborate on his testimony. "I wanted to beat up a prostitute, take my anger out on her," he confessed. "I wanted someone I can have control over. I wanted to ruin someone else's day." When Huffman's attorney, public defender Kristine Eagle, heard this new testimony, she fainted and fell to the courtroom floor.

In Harlan, Kentucky, it is unlawful to throw coal at another person—but only if the piece of coal is larger than three inches.

The Most Dangerous Game on Earth—Golf

- Scott Browning of Houston, Texas, was awarded $16,500 in damages in 1996 from the Men's Club in Houston. Browning ruptured his Achilles tendon during a club-sponsored golf tournament when an exotic dancer, assigned to be his "designated caddie" and cart driver, became so drunk she overturned their cart into a drainage canal.

- Charles Wayne Brown of Newton, Iowa, was hit in the right eye by an errant golf ball stroked by car salesman Bill Samuelson in 1982. Brown's eye suffered permanent damage, and he sued Samuelson for failing to yell "fore" before he hit the ball. The lawsuit was dismissed in 1984.

- Tom Stafford of Mission Biejo, California, sliced the ball too hard to the left, causing it to ricochet off a steel pole and crack him in the forehead. He sued the golf course for damages and in November 1993 won an $8,500 settlement.

It is illegal in Gary, Indiana, for a person to attend the theater within four hours of eating garlic.

Thanks for the Lift

There is an unusual law in Buckfield, Maine, regarding when you should and should not pay a taxicab driver. The ordinance decrees that no taxi driver "will be allowed" to ask for, or charge, a fare to any passenger who gives him or her "sexual favors" in exchange for a lift home. The law goes on to specify that the person who grants the sexual favors must be leaving an "establishment which serves alcoholic beverages," or any "place of business" which sells liquor. Even then the cab driver will probably still expect a tip.

In Cushing, Oklahoma, it is against the law to drink beer while attired only in underwear.

A Fashion Statement

The Arizona Commission on Judicial Conduct cited Magistrate Michael Lex in 1994 for violating a conduct code provision which requires judges to "act at all times in a manner that promotes public confidence in the integrity and impartiality of the judiciary." The reprimand is centered around a comment Judge Lex made to Assistant City Prosecutor Brenda Cook while she was in his courtroom. The judge didn't like the fact that Cook had worn crimson-colored pumps into his court and he exclaimed, "Only whores wear red shoes." In a written statement by the judge, Lex claimed he meant well by his comment: "I believe that, however well-intentioned my comments to the prosecutor might have been, publication of those comments out of their original context reflected poorly upon myself, my court, and all members of the judiciary." If calling someone a whore is a well-intentioned comment, I'd hate to hear one of his criticisms.

In Michigan, you are not allowed to tie your pet crocodile to a fire hydrant.

The Prison Files Part 3

Over 50,000 federal lawsuits are filed by prisoners each year. The majority of lawsuits that clog the offices of the district attorney are those filed by prisoners—for free. "Iron bars do not a prison make," but sometimes they make for young legal eagles.

● Mansfield Correctional inmates Paul B. Goist and Craig A. Anthony filed a lawsuit in Richland County, Ohio, for $20,000 against General Foods Corporation. They claimed the company was negligent in not having warning labels that list Maxwell House coffee as addictive. "I have been using Maxwell House Instant Coffee for prolong [*sic*] periods of time. Upon trying to discontinue use of said product, Maxwell House Instant Coffee, I have suffered painful withdrawal symptoms."

● A lawsuit filed by Missouri inmates claimed that a limit on Kool-Aid refills constitutes "cruel and unusual punishment."

● Kenneth D. Parker, serving time for robbery in Ely, Nevada, filed suit in U.S. District Court in Reno, alleging civil rights violations and property rights violations. Parker claimed that while he was incarcerated in Carson City, he ordered a jar of chunky peanut butter from the prison store and was given a jar of creamy peanut butter instead. He refused the creamy version and demanded his chunky. He was told the store was temporarily out of chunky, but more would be in soon. Parker was then transferred to the new state prison in Ely but his jar of chunky peanut butter never arrived. "Plaintiff is out one jar of crunchy peanut butter worth $2.50," U.S. District Judge Edward C. Reed ruled. "And should seek relief through the prison grievance system of the Nevada small-claims court." Before he dismissed the case, the judge pointed out that Parker's lawsuit had already cost several hundred dollars in court time and attorney fees.

- An inmate in New York sued for his "constitutional right" to use pink towels instead of the prison-issued white ones.

It is illegal to feed margarine, rather than real butter, to prisoners in Wisconsin.

And the Blind Shall Be Made to See

In 1995 Southeastern Guide Dogs, Inc. was a 14-year-old guide-dog school and the only company of its kind in the Southeast to raise, train, and make available at no cost to the visually impaired seeing-eye dogs. One day, Freddy, a seeing-eye dog, was leading his new master, a blind man, on a training exercise to see if the two could work together. An instructor for the company observed the team as they practiced at the Bradenton shopping mall located about 35 miles south of Tampa, Florida. A woman, Carolyn Christian, also at the mall, had stopped to watch, when the blind man accidentally stepped on her toe. Over a year after the incident, Southeastern Guide Dogs was notified that it was being sued by Christian, who claimed her toe had been broken by the blind man. Carolyn Christian sought $80,000 in damages, another $80,000 was sought by her husband, the Reverend William Christian. But according to several witnesses, Christian had made no effort to move out of the blind man's way because she had been curious "to see if the dog would walk around me." The Christians may have been trying to fill up their collection plates, but the case was dropped.

"The carrying of concealed weapons is forbidden unless same are exhibited to public view."
—a Pocatello, Idaho, law

Lawsuit Crazy

In the four-month period from November 1993 to February 1994, Brenda Butler Bryant of Philadelphia, Pennsylvania, filed a record-breaking 335 federal lawsuits. These 335 lawsuits accounted for one-fifth of all new cases filed during that time. Judge Jay Waldman, who had to read through every lawsuit, said all of Bryant's complaints were frivolous and unintelligible. Here's a sample from one of Bryant's lawsuits against the Social Security Administration: "Big Mac? Slave Master Now? No slave ain't master now. Ride them cowboy. Terrorist, radicals, and militants in authoritative roles to provoke violent crimes. Cecil B. Moor." A case like this should be named "The State of Mind versus Brenda Butler Bryant."

**It is illegal in Chicago, Illinois, to take a
French poodle to the opera.**

A Fee Circus

A lawyer from Dallas, Texas, headed a team of lawyers against Allstate and Farmers insurance companies in 1996, suing because of the companies' methods of calculating payments. According to the plaintiffs, Allstate and Farmers insurance companies increased the prices of automobile insurance premiums by rounding the prices up to the nearest even amounts. The proposed settlement, structured by the lawyers, would give the lawyer and his team of attorneys $10 million in legal fees—while policyholders would only be entitled to apply for a refund of $5.50.

In Lubbock, Texas, people are strictly forbidden from sleeping in garbage cans (even if the cans are empty).

First, Kill All the Lawyers

It is the considered opinion of this author that most lawyers are hard-working individuals who are truly concerned about justice and fair play. But this book isn't about them. This book is about the other kind of lawyers . . . you know the kind I'm talking about.

- A lawyer hurt his back while lifting and inspecting the underside of his leather office chair. He sued for workmen's compensation and was awarded $107,913.75.

- A lawyer in Los Angeles charged clients in 135 separate cases for an identical piece of legal research: the definition of a "collapsed" condominium.

- A Houston, Texas, attorney, on behalf of dozens of people, sued the manufacturers of defective plastic pipe. The settlement gave the lawyer a fee of nearly $109 million while the customers, who were the ones inconvenienced by the faulty products, received replacement plumbing valued at $1,200. The judge considered the attorney's original fee as "almost scandalous" and reduced it to a mere $43.5 million.

- A lawyer working for his state's Worker's Compensation Division threw out his back reaching for a statute book on a top shelf of the state's supreme court law library. He sued under the workmen's compensation law and was awarded $30,000.

Cats are forbidden from chasing dogs up telephone poles in International Falls, Minnesota.

More Legal History

The history behind a 12-person jury dates back to ancient days when the court astrologer chose the individual jurors. The astrologer made his selection based on each juror's astrological sign. The theory was that by having a representative from each of the 12 zodiac signs, every possible personality type would be represented, and the accused would be assured a fair trial. Hey, a fair and impartial jury—what a novel idea!

**"Intoxicated persons are prohibited from operating
a vehicle on any public highway or street,
except for a wheelbarrow."**
—a Utah ordinance

A Computer Hacker with an Ax to Grind

Shawn Kevin Quinn, then 17, had his eye on a special girl he dreamed of asking out; the only problem was she was dating someone else. Quinn, a self-confessed computer junkie, ran the problem through his head and came up with a workable solution: he would hire someone to kill the boyfriend. In 1993 the Texas teen found someone who would commit the murder for him, and they met to discuss the details. Quinn promised the hit man $5.30 and seven Atari game cartridges to zap the intruder of his dream date, and the killer accepted the terms. There was only one problem, the hit man turned out to be an undercover agent. Quinn appeared in front of District Judge Denise Collins who sentenced the teen to probation, a $500 fine, and counseling, stating the boy was very immature and not likely to be a threat to others. As the final stipulation of his probation, Judge Collins ordered Quinn to reduce the amount of time he spent in front of his computer from eight hours a day to 90 minutes. When Quinn complained about the unfairness of having his computer time docked, Judge Collins expressed her feelings, "Tough noogies!"

According to a Tallahassee, Florida, city ordinance, no train "is permitted to run through the city at a speed faster than an ordinary citizen can walk."

Straddling Defense

Every person accused of a crime is allowed to defend himself or herself, and a clever defense can convince a jury that the person either didn't commit the crime ("If the glove does not fit, you must acquit") or that the accused was somehow not responsible for their criminal actions. To wit:

● In October 1996, one day after pleading guilty to hiring a hit man, Charles S. Shapiro begged the Montgomery County, Maryland, court to allow him to change his plea. He claimed his judgment had been impaired because he had ingested tranquilizers along with an entire bottle of extra-strength Tums before he had confessed.

● Troy Matthew Gentzler confessed to tossing rocks at cars from an overpass on Interstate 83 near York, Pennsylvania. But his lawyer claimed he was the victim of "Roid rage," erratic emotional swings caused by steroid use.

● In Dodge City, Kansas, on April 16, 1991, five drunk and stoned teenagers randomly attacked and shot a 26-year-old stranger killing him on the spot. The teenagers' defense attorneys claimed their clients had been hypnotized by the Houston-based rap group, the Geto Boys. (Note: This is the first case to use music-induced insanity as a defense in a murder trial.)

According to a New York State law, "each train must be preceded by a courier afoot or on a horse," in order to announce to the citizens the approaching train.

Gone But Not Forgotten

It was a sad day for Joyce Walp and Michael Bachman when their ten-year-old Old English sheepdog, Ruffian, died. The couple took their departed loved one to the Long Island Pet Cemetery on November 4, 1989, to be laid to rest. They spent $1,083 for a headstone and burial and requested that the dog be buried with her favorite toys, a little pink blanket, and her black collar. After the funeral services, Ms. Walp and Mr. Bachman returned to their empty home to mourn. In June 1991 the couple were aghast to hear the names of the owners of the pet cemetery, Samuel Strauss and his son Alan, mentioned on the news in connection with charges of federal mail fraud and allegations that they dumped an estimated 250,000 pets in mass graves and mass cremations. Ms. Walp and Mr. Bachman rushed back to the cemetery and dug up the dog's grave—it was empty. "We were horrified," Ms. Walp said. The cemetery owners called them back two months later to show them the grave site again. This time it contained the partially decomposed body of a dog but no toys, no pink blanket, and no black collar. Ms. Walp and Mr. Bachman sued the Long Island Pet Cemetery for fraud. During their non-jury trial, Ms. Walp and Mr. Bachman both admitted they had to undergo psychological therapy because of the nightmare of their ordeal. Mr. Bachman claimed to have lost 60 pounds because of the stress. On August 31, 1992, Justice Stuart Ain of the New York State Supreme Court agreed that the pet cemetery owners had fraudulently disposed of the couple's dog and awarded the grieving couple $1.2 million in punitive and compensatory damages.

"No dog shall be in public without its master on a leash."
—a strangely phrased Belvedere, California, ordinance

Sitting in Judgment

In February 1995, in Nashville, Tennessee, Criminal Court Judge Douglas A. Meyer was suspended for 30 days for conduct unbecoming a judge. After a defendant was found not guilty of rape by reason of insanity, Judge Meyer told the man he needed to "find a girlfriend because if he doesn't, he is going to have bad dreams again" and then recommended that the public defender enroll the defendant in a dating service. And on Valentine's Day of the same year, Meyer thought it appropriate to give a female court reporter, a clerk, the assistant public defender, and an investigator, presents of red lace underwear folded into rosebud shapes. What would Clarence Thomas think?

A law in Phoenix, Arizona, deems that a male must always wear a pair of pants when he decides to come into town.

A Victim of Her Own Crime

While recuperating from a hysterectomy at Valley Lutheran Hospital in Mesa, Arizona, in February 1995, Jean K. Dooley pulled a pistol from her husband's briefcase and opened fire. Dooley's intended victim was her husband, but when her shooting spree was over, he wasn't the one injured—a nurse and paramedic had been hit instead. In January 1997, Jean Dooley filed a lawsuit against the hospital, claiming it was negligent in allowing the gun in the ward in the first place and that the shooting caused her "extreme anxiety, mental anguish, and other emotional suffering."

In Leahy, Washington, it is against the law to blow your nose in public. This ordinance was enacted because it was thought that blowing your nose in public might scare a horse and cause it to panic.

A Mother of a Lawsuit

Auto mechanic Kenneth Arrowood sued his 78-year-old mother, Hazel Arrowood, in a Georgia magistrate court in July 1991, seeking $2,613 as money due for repairing her truck. Hazel Arrowood turned around and immediately filed a countersuit, demanding more immediate relief. Her complaint read: "The plaintiff is indebted to the defendant for 40 years of services rendered as a mother, guidance counselor, cook, maid, banker, nurse, bail bondswoman, baby-sitter, laundry worker, and psychologist, all of which the plaintiff has not paid for." It went on to read, "As a mother, and provided the law will allow me, I would publicly give my son the whipping that he so rightly needs and which I failed to give him as a child." In case the judge wouldn't allow her to whip her son, Hazel's pleading gave an alternative. She asked that the court "appoint a bailiff or other court official to apply to my son the hickory whipping." Hazel Arrowood won the lawsuit, but the judge declined to allow Hazel or anyone else to spank Kenneth.

It is against the law in Oxford, Ohio, for a woman to take off her clothing while standing in front of a picture of a man.

Sidelined by the Law

A Tucson, Arizona, statute reads: "It shall be unlawful for any visiting football team or player to carry, convey, tote, kick, throw, pass or otherwise transport or propel any inflated pigskin across the University of Arizona goal line or score a safety within the confines of the city of Tucson, County of Pina, State of Arizona." Violators can be fined $300 and sentenced to not less than three months in the city jail.

**It is against the law in Green Bay, Wisconsin, for a car to drip oil on the pavement.
The penalty is $1 per drip.**

Give the Defense a Rest!

It is the goal of some trial lawyers to set precedents in their work, citing defenses that have never before been used. Sometimes these strategies work and sometimes they don't—and some of them are very strange. Here are a few of the more unique defenses recently used in American courts.

• "Urban Survival Syndrome"—The lawyer for Daimion Osby, a black 18-year-old who shot two unarmed blacks in a Fort Worth parking lot in 1993, deadlocked the jury after he argued that Osby suffered from "urban survival syndrome"—a fear that inner-city residents have of other people in their same area.

• "The Twinkie Defense"—On November 27, 1978, Dan White, a former police officer and a member of San Francisco's board of supervisors, shot to death the city's mayor, George Moscone, and Harvey Milk, the board's first openly gay supervisor. White's attorneys brought in a team of psychiatrists who each attempted to explain why White had murdered the two men. One psychiatrist delved into White's junk-food addiction, especially to Twinkies, Coca-Cola, and potato chips. He explained that because of all the junk food White had consumed, his blood-sugar levels might have compounded his manic depression and contributed to the killings. On May 21, 1979, White was convicted of involuntary manslaughter. He later committed suicide.

• A potential legal defense is being considered by a group of professionals who failed to file their income tax returns on time. They claim they suffer from an anxiety syndrome characterized by "an overall inability to act in [their] own interest." According to a psychiatry professor, victims are "highly ambitious, hypercritical, detail-oriented people," who cannot relax, don't trust others to do work assigned to them, and have a tendency to procrastinate and become secretive.

- "Black rage" was the defense used by Colin Ferguson, who is black, to explain why he killed four whites and two Asian-Americans on a Long Island Railroad train. This syndrome is a type of insanity caused by prolonged racial prejudice in the United States. Ferguson is Jamaican.

In Rumford, Maine, it is illegal to bite your landlord.

Like a Bolt Out of the Blue

Scott Abrams, then 27, filed a lawsuit in April 1993 against the managers and owners of an apartment building in Arlington, Virginia, seeking $2 million in damages. Abrams claims the management was negligent in maintaining the rooftop and should have placed signs and used brighter paint to warn him of the possible dangers incurred by his actions. Abrams's demands stem from a 1991 accident in which he had been sitting on the ledge of the roof with his feet in a puddle, during an electric storm, and was struck by lightning. I guess the sign should read "Hey, Idiot, Watch Out!"

It is illegal in North Carolina for a farmer to plow his field using an elephant.

As God Is My Witness

In November 1993 the atmosphere in the Independent Baptist Church in Hillsboro, Illinois, was electrifying. Reverend Anthony Dearinger was teaching from the book of Revelations, preaching hellfire and damnation. Overcome by the Holy Spirit, and needing a visual aid to show how God will toss Satan into hell on Judgment Day, Reverend Dearinger plucked an eight-year-old boy out of the congregation and threw him down the aisle. A witness estimated the boy flew "a good six feet" through the air before landing beside one of the back pews. As penance for his transgression, the Reverend was sentenced in 1994 to two years of court supervision and 200 hours of community service. Reverend Dearinger's congregation is now very careful when it asks him to "pass the plate."

The law in Groton, Connecticut, states that "any utterances from a man in a bow tie are not to be credited."

Walking Abreast with the IRS

Cynthia Hess, an exotic dancer who goes by the stage name "Chesty Love," submitted herself to "multiple medical procedures" to augment her bust size to a mind-boggling 56FF. Not only did she double her bra size (her breasts now weigh ten pounds apiece), she nearly doubled her weekly income, from $416 a week to $750 a week. Chesty is certainly good with numbers and decided that because she had had surgery to increase her income, she could include her breasts as a business asset (or assets) and depreciate them from her gross income. The Internal Revenue Service disagreed with the buxom Indiana native and disallowed her $2,088 depreciation, citing that enhancements to health or appearance are personal and therefore not considered business expenses.

But Special Trial Judge Joan Seitz Pate decided to stick her nose into Chesty's breast business and reversed the IRS decision in March 1993. The judge concluded that Chesty's breasts were "detrimental to her health and contorted her body into a grotesque appearance, all for the purpose of money. Thus," said the judge, "even though the implants were surgically made a part of her body, we are convinced that they are not inherently personal in nature." The IRS decided not to go tit-for-tat with the judge and backed off Chesty's breasts.

It is illegal in Oak Park, Illinois, to cook more than 100 doughnuts in a single day.

Driven to Excess

Dr. Ira Gore, Jr., of Birmingham, Alabama, was delighted with his brand-new $40,000 1990 BMW. He drove it everywhere and lovingly polished and fussed over it. One day he decided to take the "Beemer" to a detailing shop to make it look a little "snazzier." The news he received from one of the shop attendants made his heart skip a beat. Apparently a portion of his beloved BMW had been repainted before he had bought it. The evidence was clear—a four-inch tape line on one of the fenders. It is a common practice among car manufacturers to have a refinishing facility touch up cars which might have received minimal damage in transit and restore them to factory conditions. According to BMW's policy, if the cost of the repair exceeds 3% of the retail price of the car, the auto is used only as a company car and then later sold as a used car. This is a common practice and, in fact, the 3% threshold BMW maintains is one of the strictest in the country. Dr. Gore decided to sue BMW for fraud and breach of contract.

Gore's lawyer did some quick calculating before arriving at a settlement offer. He deduced that even a perfectly refinished car was diminished in value by 10%; so that's $4,000. They asked for $4,000 in compensatory damages—fair enough. But approximately 1,000 cars had been touched up by BMW over the previous ten years. Gore's lawyer decided to sue for those people, too. Gore asked for punitive damages of $4 million for the minor restoration done to his car. During the trial, Gore's lawyer pleaded with the jury to award Gore the $4 million on behalf of the 1,000 innocent BMW owners who were unaware anything was wrong with their cars. The jury took one look at the doctor sitting before it, who had shelled out $40,000 for his car and now wanted $4 million, and then decided he should get it—the $4 million, that is.

The case was appealed to the Alabama Supreme Court; it ruled that $4 million was too much money for a four-inch tape line, so he was awarded what it considered a "reasonable" amount. Poor Dr. Gore received only $2 million for the terrible injustice done to him. The highest court in Alabama admitted its ruling violated BMW's right of due process by holding BMW liable for cars refinished outside of Alabama. The court thought it was fair to fine BMW for their actions in 21 other states where BMW's restoration policy met current standards. In essence, BMW was being punished for obeying the law. BMW argued that only 14 of their cars had been refurbished and sold in Alabama within the last ten years. Too bad, said the Alabama Supreme Court, give the man his $2 million. In 1995 the U.S. Supreme Court threw its act into gear and threw out the $2 million award, to which *The Wall Street Journal* commented, "[This decision was] the first time in decades that the justices actually struck down such an award as excessive."

It is against the law to burp or sneeze in church in Omaha, Nebraska.

Divorce—The Second Time Around

There are always two sides to every story during a divorce proceeding.

• A man in Smelterville, Idaho, filed for divorce because, his claim stated, "His wife dressed up as a ghost and tried to scare his elderly mother out of the house."

• A man in Honolulu, Hawaii, asked for a divorce because his wife "served pea soup for breakfast and dinner . . . and packed his lunch with pea sandwiches."

• A man in Winthrop, Maine, divorced his wife because she "wore earplugs whenever his mother came to visit."

• A woman in Lunch Heights, Delaware, filed for divorce because her husband "regularly put itching powder in her underwear when she wasn't looking."

• A woman in Frackville, Pennsylvania, filed for divorce citing the fact that her husband insisted on "shooting tin cans off her head with a slingshot."

In Atlanta, Georgia, a child can be arrested if he or she makes faces at other children during study period in a school classroom.

Driving Under the Influence

"Whoever operates an automobile or motorcycle on any public way—laid out under authority of law recklessly or while under the influence of liquor shall be punished; thereby imposing upon the motorist the duty of finding out at his peril whether certain highways had been laid out recklessly or while under the influence of liquor before driving his car over them."
—*a Massachusetts state ordinance*

If you leave your elephant tied to a parking meter in Orlando, Florida, you must put the proper amount of money in the meter for the time the elephant is there.

More Lawyers You Love to Hate

• In August 1992 a California attorney filed a $2 million lawsuit against a major gasoline company and a local Escondido gas station manager for discrimination. The attorney claimed the practice of having gas station attendants pump gas at self-service pumps for female customers was discriminatory against men who had to pump their own gas. The suit was settled out of court with the gas station agreeing to stop its chivalrous activities, forcing women to pump their own gas themselves.

• A Saint Louis, Missouri, man argued that the reason the jury found him guilty of stealing court documents was that it had been prejudiced against him. The man claimed he was demonized because the judge allowed the jury to learn his occupation—he was a lawyer.

**"Cab drivers may not knowingly carry a person
of questionable or bad character
to his or her destination."**
—*a Magnolia, Arkansas, ordinance*

Three Strikes and You're Out!

In May 1995 Kevin Weber, then 35, a parolee with two prior convictions for burglary, broke into a closed restaurant in Santa Ana, California, through a vent in the roof. Once inside, he stuffed his pockets with merchandise, returned to the roof, and was promptly arrested. Orange County Superior Court Judge Jean Rheinheimer said in October 1995 that California's "three-strikes" law left her no choice but to impose a life sentence, with a minimum of 26 years to be served. But Orange County Deputy Public Defender Deborah Barnum disagreed. Barnum claimed Weber's offense should have been considered a misdemeanor. "She could have given him one year. . . . Neither his record nor the crime warrant the life, minimum 26-year sentence." What did Weber do? He stole four cookies from the restaurant. "That's six and a half years per cookie," said Barnum. Murderers get out on early parole, and cookie thieves get a life sentence—that's why it's called just desserts.

It is illegal to advertise on tombstones in Roanoke, Virginia.

The Jury Is Now Excused

If you wish to be excused from jury duty, you have to give the judge a convincing reason. "I have to work," or "I don't feel well" won't remove you from your civil duty. Here are some of the more creative excuses given to judges:

● "I will be in space that day." This excuse was given by a real astronaut in Harris County District Court in Houston, Texas. The jury duty was rescheduled, and the astronaut was asked to return after splashdown.

● "I can't keep a secret." This was an excuse given to Judge B. Michael Dann of Arizona by a blabbermouth trying to avoid jury duty.

● In January 1995 Pamela Baker asked a Beaufort, South Carolina, judge to excuse her from jury duty in a murder trial. She claimed her husband, Baptist pastor Karl Baker, forbid her to speak in public.

Other excuses include:

● "I have to feed my bird during the day."

● "My poodle's in heat."

● "I shot holes in my daughter's boyfriend's car."

Court clerk Charles Bascarisse of Houston, remarked, "We only collect them. The judges have to rule on them."

**According to an Oregon law, it is illegal for a
dead person to serve on a jury.**

You're Outta There!!!

In 1993 Henry H. Craighead, coach of a woman's softball team, filed a $4 million lawsuit against the city of Roanoke, Virginia, claiming that his constitutional right to the pursuit of happiness was denied when he was thrown out of a game. Craighead also claimed the umpire disqualified his team from an upcoming game on the unfounded grounds that the team didn't have enough players. The lawsuit, filed in Roanoke Circuit Court, claimed Craighead was "harassed, intimidated and embarrassed." After the expulsion he suffered "great mortification, humiliation, shame, vilification, exposure to public infamy, injury to his good reputation, and has been and will forever be hampered in his pursuit of happiness."

"You can quote me as laughing," said City Attorney Wilburn Dibling. "The courts don't exist for the purpose of reviewing the actions of umpires in amateur sports contests. I think this reflects a sad commentary on the overemphasis of what are supposed to be games." Unfortunately, this doesn't constitute one strike in the "three-strikes" law.

In California you are not allowed to plant a garden in a cemetery.

It's Written in the Stars

James Blakely, a Sagittarian, filed a 19-page handwritten lawsuit against the Detroit Newspaper Agency in March 1992. The suit, filed in the Wayne County Circuit Court, demanded that both the *Detroit Free Press* and the *Detroit News* eliminate their horoscope columns and give Blakely $9 million for the pain and suffering astrology had caused him. Blakely, who acted as his own counsel, claimed 27 different charges including conspiracy, sin, defamation of character, consulting the movement of heavenly bodies, and the ruination of his marriage. "It's apparent from the complaint that the guy's a space cadet. . . . He's claiming that he was following the horoscopes, and that they messed up his private life," says John A. Taylor, in-house counsel for the two Detroit newspapers. Blakely contended that horoscopes are a consumer fraud, the work of Satan, and have caused him "an enormous amount of problems" because they predict events which will not occur.

The city of Toledo, Ohio, has made it illegal to throw any type of reptile at another person.

Age Appropriate

In December 1995, a New York City federal jury awarded Joyce Stratton $1 million in her lawsuit against the New York City Department for the Aging. Stratton, 61, who had worked with the agency for 21 years as director of the Central Information and Referral Bureau, was fired, thereby denying her a $51,000-a-year salary and her pension benefits—the agency then hired a younger person.

In Cleveland, Ohio, it is against the law to ride a bicycle with your hands off the handlebars.

Please Drive Safely

In Pennsylvania, "Any motorist driving along a country road at night must stop every mile and send up a rocket signal, wait ten minutes for the road to be cleared of livestock, and then continue." The statute goes on to declare: "Any motorist who sights a team of horses coming towards him must pull well off the road, cover his car with a blanket or canvas that blends with the countryside, and let the horses pass. If the horses appear skittish, the motorist must take his car apart, piece by piece, and hide it under the nearest bushes."

**Drivers of automobiles are forbidden
to run out of gas in Youngstown, Ohio.**

Judgment Daze #2

Getting tough on crime is always a battle cry for politicians during election time. Here are some judges who took the battle cry to heart.

• The highest bail ever set was for Jeffrey Marsh, Juan Mercado, Yolanda Kravitz, and Alvin Kravitz, who were accused of armed robbery. The presiding judge, David L. Tobin, and the four defense attorneys at the Dade County Courthouse, in Miami, Florida, set their bail on October 16, 1989 at $100 billion.

• Charles Scott Robinson was found guilty of six counts of rape of a three-year-old girl. The jury sentenced him to serve 5,000 years in prison for each of the six counts, to be served consecutively. Pattye Wallace, Oklahoma City prosecutor, said, "I don't know if we'll get more 30,000 year sentences or not, but [this one] was deserved."

• In May 1995 Leon Taylor, convicted of murdering a man during a 1994 robbery in Kansas City, Missouri, was sentenced to death, plus life in prison, with an additional 315 years tacked on.

**It is against the law in Liberty Corner, New Jersey, to honk your car horn while you're having sex.
Beep, beep!**

Jury Pool and Gene Pool

According to prosecutor Ron Davis, in July 1996 an entire 86-member jury pool, gathered for an attempted murder trial in Centerville, Tennessee (population 16,000), had to be dismissed because too many jury members were related to each other. "We had clumps of people who all lived together," said Assistant District Attorney Ron Davis. "We had brothers, cousins, sisters, mamas, and children. It became apparent that we were going to have a problem." Defense attorney Gary Howell said this was a first for him. "At one point, we had a man and his son sitting next to each other and Mama was sitting behind them," Howell said. I guess some jury members weren't sure if they were attending a trial or a family reunion.

Sparks, Nevada, ordinance reads: "A citizen is forbidden to drive a donkey along Main Street in August without a straw hat being worn." But *who* should be wearing the hat?

Straight Shooting Judge

During his hearing on a probation violation in May 1991, Gordon Meyette, then 43, spoke up in his own defense, which is against court procedure. Presiding Judge J. Leonard Fleet reprimanded Meyette and warned him not to speak again. Meyette turned to a bailiff and muttered, "If I had a gun, I'd kill that judge." Judge Fleet overheard the mumbled threat, reached into his desk, pulled out a .38-caliber revolver, and handed it to Meyette. "Do you want to take your best shot?" asked the judge. "If you're going to take a shot, you had better score because I don't miss." Meyette was speechless—which is all the judge wanted in the first place. Later, Judge Fleet explained the pistol had not been loaded and agreed there were probably better ways of dealing with loudmouths. "Perhaps it would have been more discreet had I devised some other method to get my message across to those who so frequently show disrespect for law and order," he said. The judge was soon transferred from the criminal division to the civil division. Surely Meyette will think twice before he shoots his mouth off again, especially if someone else is willing to do it for him.

**It is illegal in Hillsboro, Oregon, to allow your horse
to ride around in the backseat of your car.**

Court Jester

In 1993 the California Commission on Judicial Performance publicly repremanded the behavior of Judge Gary Friedman, a San Francisco Superior Court Judge. Apparently, Judge Friedman thought it would be funny to send an inmate, who had an intense fear of snakes, the severed head of a rattlesnake. The Superior Court-Jester also must have thought it was witty to send a publicity photo of a female movie star, to which he added a personalized yet phony inscription, to another defendant who was facing charges of stalking the starlet. Friedman issued a formal apology: "I at no time intended to demean in any way the two inmates on trial before me," he said. "I sincerely apologize for any perception to the contrary." The commission went no further in its discipline of Judge Friedman other than the public reproval, explaining that "humor can assist in humanizing the otherwise intimidating atmosphere of our courts." Also it felt justified in its leniency because Judge Friedman sent the rattler head and the headshot of the star six years ago and "did not repeat the incidents."

**In Massachusetts one is not allowed to lounge
on shelves in a bakery.**

Nope to the Pope

It was a case that rocked Texas. A Catholic priest from San Antonio was accused of child abuse. Michelle Petty, the attorney for the child, argued that not only was the priest liable, so was his employer (i.e., the Catholic Church). In a 1976 ruling, the Supreme Court allowed for an employees' boss to be held liable for the actions of their employees. Petty claimed that, according to this ruling, she should be allowed to name as a defendant—the Pope. U.S. Attorney Michael Buckholz argued, however, that Pope John Paul II had immunity because he is not only the head of the Catholic Church, he is also a head of state, the Vatican. On March 15, 1994, a judge in San Antonio ruled that coming to Texas would not be the Pope's cross to bear and that he could not be named in the suit.

According to an ordinance in Okanogah, Washington, burglars "can steal only after dark."

Have a Nice Day

In July 1992, when the Honorable Charles J. Hearn of Houston, Texas, 263rd judicial district, signed an order setting the execution date for Robert Nelson Drew, he added a little something extra to his signature—a happy face. "If Fidel Castro, for example, signed death warrants with happy faces, the United States would demand that the United Nations commence hostilities against the Cuban dictator," said Drew's lawyer, New York attorney Ron Kuby. "We'd point to it as an example of the depraved barbarism of this individual." William M. Kunstler, the well-known liberal lawyer, who worked with Kuby, said Drew was more outraged than cheered by the happy face. "It's like he's saying 'Have a nice death,'" said Kunstler. Both attorneys confessed that the happy face complaint is "actually the last issue [Drew] has" to fight the execution since he has exhausted appeals on other issues. Now retired, Judge Hearn said he meant no disrespect to Drew, who was convicted of the stabbing death of an Alabama teen; it's just his way of symbolizing his born-again Christian faith and his positive outlook on life. "It's that simple. I'm a happy person," said Hearn. "I thought it was just a nice touch to the signature, and it makes people smile." Hearn confessed to signing most documents with a happy face, including other death warrants. The happy face is "not intended to take away from the seriousness of anything. It's just become part of my signature. My driver's license is signed that way." Hearn went on to say, "We've got too many people walking around this world with grim looks on their faces." Since Hearn signed the happy face on other death warrants, we know certain people won't be walking around with grim looks on their faces much longer.

It is illegal in Brooklyn, New York, for a donkey
to sleep in a bathtub.

Deflowers in Washington

You can't have sex with a virgin in the state of Washington—even if you marry her. It's the law. The wording of this ordinance is such that it is a major crime to deflower a virgin, even if she is your wife. The law reads: "Every person who shall seduce and have sexual intercourse with any female of previously chaste character shall be punished by imprisonment in the state penitentiary for not more than five (5) years or in the county jail for not more than one (1) year or by a fine of $1000 or by both fine and imprisonment."

It is illegal in Saint Point, Idaho, for any person over the age of 88 to ride a motorcycle.

Quick Convict Cases #3

- In April 1996 the Iowa Supreme Court prevented inmate Kirk Livingood from suing his cell mate, Phillip Negrete. Livingood wanted to sue Negrete, who he claims routinely beat him, under the state's domestic-abuse law.

- Convicted rapist, robber, and kidnapper Melvin Leroy Tyler, serving time in Missouri, filed a lawsuit for $129 million to have prisoners supplied with a salad bar and brunches on weekends and holidays.

- A New York City inmate sued for $8.5 million in damages because he smuggled a gun into the prison and then accidentally shot himself.

- Richard Loritz filed a $2,000 lawsuit against the South Bay Detention Center in San Diego, California, for refusing to allow him to use dental floss.

It is against the law in New York State to shoot at a rabbit from the back end of a Third Avenue streetcar while it is in motion.

If at First You Don't Succeed

It was a proud day when 61-year-old Maxcy Dean Filer, a member of the Compton, California, City Council, finally passed the California Bar Exam. "I cried happily and hugged all my children and my wife," Filer exclaimed. Filer had long dreamed of being a lawyer, but for years had to settle for the position of part-time clerk for one of his two lawyer sons. "I can stop washing windows, and I have to pay bar dues," said the new lawyer. Filer first took the bar exam in 1967 and finally passed it 24 years later in 1991—after failing it 47 times.

Citizens of Brewton, Alabama, are not allowed to "drive a motorboat" on a city street. It is also illegal for anyone to fish from a motorboat while it is being driven down any street or highway in the city.

Frozen Assets

In 1994 a Los Angeles superior court judge ruled that Deborah Ellen Hecht, then 39, would finally get a small but important part of her ex-lover William E. Kane's estate. Kane committed suicide in October 1991 and Hecht had been waging a legal battle with Kane's former wife, Sandra McMahan Irwin, and their two grown children over dispensation of a portion of the inheritance. What was the item in contention? Sperm. Before his suicide, Kane donated 15 vials of sperm to a sperm bank which Hecht claims were deposited on her account. Irwin and the two children argued that Kane was obviously not of sound mind when he promised Hecht the sperm, using as an example the fact that he killed himself shortly thereafter. But on March 28, 1994, Judge Arnold Gold ruled that Hecht would receive three of the 15 vials of sperm since a settlement agreement gave her 20 percent of Kane's property. "Deborah's obviously very happy because she wants to have this baby," Hecht's attorney, Marvin Rudnick of Pasadena, was quoted as saying. "We're just happy that the future of procreation is alive and well in the courts." Hecht, of Santa Monica, California, paid the estate $60 for early withdrawal of the sperm and promised not to claim another part of the estate if she has a baby. The decision raises an interesting legal question—would a child conceived and born after the death of the father or mother be entitled to a portion of the parent's estate? The answer: coming soon to a courthouse near you.

**It is against the law in Hawaii to insert
pennies into your ears.**

A Bad Judge of Character

Former State Appeals Court Judge Charles Galbreath of Nashville, Tennessee, made a terrible error in judgment in 1995 when the "hitchhiker" he picked up one morning walking down Eighth Avenue North turned out to be a transvestite prostitute. But this drag queen wasn't a hooker with a heart of gold; he stole $20 from the former judge and ran away. "She said, 'I got a pimp waiting for me,'" Galbreath recalled. "'If you don't give me $20, he's going to beat me up.'" The lawyer said he searched for a $20 bill, found one, and handed it over. The transvestite then got out of the car and walked away. "She was the most considerate robber I've ever heard of," Galbreath said. Galbreath confessed that even though the passenger, Lamont E. Hayes, offered to have sex with him for money, he refused, claiming "she was too damn ugly."

**New York passed a law that makes it illegal
to do anything illegal.**

Defendants Say the Damnedest Things

The law allows for a person accused of a crime to speak in his or her own behalf. Sometimes the individuals apologize, sometimes they try to explain their situation, and sometimes they stick their foot in their mouths.

- "I object to your calling me a person, your honor."
—*Rodney Skurdal, member of the Freemen on June 14, 1996, when asked by a federal magistrate if he had the right person before him*

- "What are you talking about, some 'witness,' man? There was only me and her in the store."
—*Jeffrey Johnson, on trial for robbing a Texaco station in Wilmington, Delaware. Johnson claimed to be elsewhere during the crime and blurted out this statement in objection to testimony by a police officer who accidentally used the term "witness" instead of "victim."*

- "I enjoyed drinking while driving. It's one of the most pleasurable habits I've had."
—*Steven L. Johnson, then 40, explaining his situation to the judge who had just sentenced him to two years in prison in Brooking, South Dakota, in 1992*

You are not allowed to mistreat an oyster in Baltimore.

Some Like It Hot

Some people like spicy food, but how hot is too hot? How much added spice constitutes a criminal assault? That was the question in front of Judge Albert J. Cirone, Jr., of Lebanon, New Hampshire. In February 1994 Michael Towne, a cook at a local Denny's restaurant in West Lebanon, prepared ham-and-egg sandwiches for two Vermont state troopers. The troopers turned into real "Smoky Bears" when their mouths felt like a forest fire—their sandwiches had been dressed with Tabasco sauce. The two troopers arrested Towne, who claimed to be innocent, and charged him with criminal assault. When the case appeared before Judge Cirone on June 6, 1996, he put the lid on the Tabascoed troopers by interpreting the New Hampshire statute defining assault as "unprivileged *physical* contact." In his opinion, Judge Cirone wrote, "One officer ate his entire meal and the other ate substantially all of his meal. At some point in their consumption of the food their conduct amounted to a consent to the contact of the Tabasco with their palate." The judge went on to write, "Additionally, to allow this case to go forward would require the court to enunciate a standard based on personal tastes to establish the point at which a legal condiment becomes an instrument to carry out an assault." This case may go down in the books as "assault with a dangerous pepper."

A law in Chicago bans people from eating in an establishment that is on fire.

Kitten Caboodle

John David Celinski, then 33, a NASA subcontractor from Houston, Texas, was found guilty of misdemeanor animal cruelty following testimony by his former girlfriend, Sheryl Jones. Celinski confessed to the Harris County District Court on September 8, 1994, that he was jealous of Jones's two cats, Sugar Ray and Bonnie. Celinski did the only thing he could think of to show Jones his jealous nature; he gave the felines doses of the pain reliever acetaminophen, then microwaved them to death. He was fined $1,800 and two years' probation. Not an extremely severe punishment considering Celinski took 18 lives.

In Philadelphia, Mississippi, it is illegal for any man, woman, or child to participate in a barking competition with a dog.
Breaking this law could bring a $10 fine for "insulting public behavior."

The Devil Made Me Do It

In yet another example of prisoners having too much time on their hands, Gerald Mayo, an inmate at a Pennsylvania state correctional facility, filed a lawsuit against "Satan and his staff." In *United States ex rel. Gerald Mayo v. Satan And His Staff* (United States District Court, W.D. Pennsylvania, Dec. 3, 1971), Mayo sought permission to sue Satan for civil rights violations. Mayo claimed that Satan and his staff had, on numerous occasions, caused plaintiff (Mayo) misery and unwarranted threats, placed deliberate obstacles in his path, and caused his downfall and his subsequent incarceration. District Judge Weber, after thoughtful deliberation, came to the following conclusions about Mr. Mayo's lawsuit. 1) That the defendant (Satan) was not a resident of the state of Pennsylvania. 2) That the plaintiff "failed to include with his complaint the required form of instructions for the United States Marshall for directions as to" where Satan lives in order to serve him/her papers. Judge Weber concluded, "For the foregoing reasons we must exercise our discretion to refuse the prayer of plaintiff to proceed in" the lawsuit. I guess Judge Weber figured Mayo would have a devil of a time proving his claim.

**It is illegal in Vermont to deny the existence of God.
Atheists can be fined up to $200.**

Greenwich Mean Time

In Texas the federally funded organization Advocacy, Inc., which promotes the rights of the disabled, sued the Austin-Travis County Mental Health and Mental Retardation Center in 1994—for getting up too early. The lawsuit forced the center to change the time of its board meetings from 8 AM to no earlier than 9 AM. Is it me or does the phrase "the patients are running the asylum" leap to mind?

It is against the law in Phoenix, Arizona, to put glass bottles under a horse's hooves.

Small-Town Justice

As a joke, Justin Weaver of Randolph, New York, wrote his own name on the ballot for town justice during the November 3, 1992, elections. The 21-year-old headed back to work on the family farm and forgot about his little prank—until the election results came in. Weaver, who ran uncontested in the race, won by a 1-to-0 vote and was elected as town justice for a one-year term. "It's really taught me that one vote does make a difference," said Justice Justin. When Justin received his judging certificate in January 1993, which allowed him to practice law, he didn't exactly run his robe up the flagpole in celebration. Justin, who had no training in law, had to read a thick manual, which he judged to be about 600 pages, and attend classes, which weren't scheduled to be held until the end of March. Until he got this formal education, Justin decided it would be best not to hold court. Town officials, who had been trying to eliminate the position of town justice, wrangled over the problem of a salary for Justin. They offered him $30 a week for the position, but Weaver wanted to earn what the other justice was making—over $8,000 a year. Becoming the town justice has renewed Justin's interest in education, and he said he would like to return to the University of Wyoming, which he previously attended for one year, to earn a degree in either law or earth sciences.

In Michigan it is against the law to put a skunk in your boss's desk.

Taking a Notch Out of the Bible Belt

In April 1993, "U–John, King Priest of the Universal Sovereign" filed an 11-page lawsuit in U.S. District Court in Atlanta, seeking $10 trillion against 36 Bible-based religions for a century's worth of "fraud, breach of duty, global disruption of peace, slander, defamation of the divine character, blasphemy, and wanton greed."

Hey, U–John, judge not lest ye be judged.

A Cicero, Illinois, law states that whenever there is more than three inches of snow in the city, a "street must be cleared of all vehicles or be towed away."

Evidence Kept
Under Wraps

In September 1988 Edward Vasquez, a criminal justice and sociology student at California State University in Los Angeles, was arrested for the shooting death of a security guard in a central Los Angeles parking lot. Witnesses described the perpetrator as wearing a white T-shirt, but Vasquez claimed he had been wearing his green jacket at the time. Vasquez admitted to being in the general vicinity during the murder, but claimed he had been on the other side of the parking lot, buying a burrito from a canteen truck vendor. During his cross-examination, Vasquez claimed he had been hit in the buttocks by a stray bullet and that's when the prosecution had jumped on his case. If, as Vasquez claimed, he had been hit with a bullet and he had been wearing his green jacket at the time, the jacket should show definite blood stains. The jacket, which had been locked away in the evidence room for nearly two years, was brought out and the examination proved that there were not even trace amounts of blood on it. Jay Jaffe, Vasquez's lawyer, argued that the jacket only reached to Vasquez's waist and handed the jacket to Vasquez to try on in front of the jury. It did indeed only go to his waist. While the jury was in the deliberating room deciding Vasquez's fate, Vasquez told his lawyer that when he had tried the jacket on he had felt "something heavy in the right pocket." The jurors were asked to reenter the courtroom and take their seats as the jacket was brought back before them. Jaffe reached into the right pocket in full view of the jury and pulled out an item wrapped in aluminum foil. The foil was slowly peeled away and a rotten, rancid, two-year-old burrito was uncovered. Vasquez was acquitted.

A Los Angeles, California, ordinance makes it against
the law for any person to have a hippopotamus
in his possession.

Mounting a Defense

The Florida heat must have gotten the better of tiny Rocky, a Chihuahua belonging to Dayami Diaz. Rocky spied a powerful female rottweiler named Canella tied to the back deck of her owner Devin Foley's home. Foley had just stepped inside to get Canella a little kibble to munch on. That's when the attack, amorous though it might have been, took place. Rocky, feeling that no mountain was high enough to climb, mounted Canella and had his way with her. According to Monroe County Judge Reagan Rtomey, "A passing animal control officer observed Canella and Rocky passionately joined together and 'stopped to watch because of the difference in sizes' of the two dogs." Foley ran inside and got a camera to take a picture of the scene, while the animal control agent turned a garden hose on the passionate pooches to break their love connection. Foley sued Rocky's owner, Diaz, claiming Canella's virtue had been kept pure so she could be bred to "an acceptable male so that a litter might be sold." One month later, Rocky had reason to brag about his conquest because Canella was pregnant. During the trial in 1994, Diaz presented character witnesses who shed a dark light on Canella's alleged chastity. Several neighbors testified that other dogs in the neighborhood had also "known" Canella, including a petite shih tzu with an injured hip. Even so, Diaz was ordered to pay Foley $2,567.50 for the loss of Canella's future "acceptable" breeding possibilities. There is no word if Rocky has made any "pup support" payments.

**In Joplin, Missouri, it is illegal to give a dog
a drink of whiskey.**

The Prison Files Part 4

This is the final installment of outlaw lawsuits.

- William Warren, who is serving a life sentence in Oklahoma's Joseph Harp Correctional Center, has filed a lawsuit claiming "cruel and unusual punishment" because prison officials make him wear regulation white cotton underwear. Talk about setting yourself up for "cruel and unusual punishment," Warren wants the right to wear women's nylon bikini panties.

- Lawrence Bittaker, a serial killer on death row, was convicted in 1979 of the sexual assault, torture, and mutilation murders of five teenage girls in Los Angeles County. In 1992 he filed a lawsuit claiming "cruel and unusual punishment" because prison guards served him soggy sandwiches and broken cookies in his sack lunches. The lawsuit was finally dismissed as frivolous after Deputy Attorney General Jim Humes spent thousands of dollars to prove to the judge that, even if Bittaker refused to eat his sack lunch, the prison breakfast and dinner contained more than enough calories to keep him alive—at least until the state finally carries out his sentence.

- One Indiana inmate is seeking damages because the meat and vegetables on his dinner plate were "somewhat mixed together" one night.

It is illegal in Oklahoma to get a fish drunk.

➡

Fast-Food Fool

Timothy Ray Anderson, with a stocking pulled over his head, burst into a McDonald's restaurant in Milwaukee, Wisconsin, and pointed his pistol at the manager's face. He then jumped over the counter and was emptying the cash register when security guard John Hobson ordered Anderson to drop his gun. Anderson spun around and aimed, but Hobson shot first and hit the would-be robber in the stomach. At his trial, Anderson was convicted of armed robbery and sentenced to 15 years in prison. From his jail cell, Anderson filed a lawsuit against Hobson, the security company Hobson worked for, and the McDonald's owner, claiming "excessive force" was used against him. Scott Anderson, Anderson's attorney, but no relation, told the *Milwaukee Journal:* "The mere fact that you're holding up a McDonald's with a gun doesn't mean you give up your right to be protected from somebody who wants to shoot you." A judge threw the case out of court.

It is against the law to throw onions at anyone in Princeton, Texas.

Hoop in Mouth Disease

When Christopher Conley of Nashua, New Hampshire, was playing a game of basketball, he charged the hoop, went up for a slam dunk, and got more hang time than he expected—his teeth got entangled in the net on the way down. The 14-year-old went straight from the basketball court to a court of law. Conley and his parents sued Lifetime Products, the makers of the net, seeking damages for the cost of Christopher's extensive dental work. Lifetime Products settled with the Conleys in November 1995, and Christopher's technical foul netted him $50,000.

According to a local ordinance in Newburgh, New York, no one is allowed to eat popcorn or peanuts while walking backward when there is a concert in progress.

Your Own Worst Enemy

On March 23, 1993, George Marquardt was called before U.S. District Judge Patrick Kelly in Wichita, Kansas. Judge Kelly called the hearing to discuss why Marquardt, accused of manufacturing a heroin substitute called fentanyl, refused to accept a lawyer's help and chose to defend himself. The judge got some surprising answers to his routine questions. The exchange went like this:

KELLY: Until you were arrested, what was your employment?

MARQUARDT: Drug manufacturer.

KELLY: What?

MARQUARDT: Drug manufacturer.

KELLY: What kind of drugs?

MARQUARDT: Clandestine.

KELLY: In other words, your mode of occupation was engag[ing] in illegal manufacture of controlled substances?

MARQUARDT: It was. I fixed an instrument every now and then, a mass spectrometer, things like that, but mostly manufactured drugs.

Upon hearing Marquardt's answers, Assistant U.S. Attorney Blair Watson said, "He's a most articulate gentleman. I think he was simply answering the court's questions."

It is against the law in Ohio to ride a jackass faster than the legal speed limit of six miles per hour.

Landing in the Rough

After a hard day on the links, Dale L. Larson was headed back to the club-house at the Indianhead golf course in Wausau, Wisconsin, when he tripped on his golf spikes and fell face first onto the brick path. It took nine root canals and 23 dental crowns to get Larson's smile back to normal. Larson was so teed off that he sued the golf course for damages. During the trial, the jury agreed that the golf course was 51 percent responsible for Larson's accident. They concluded that had the path been made of smooth concrete, Larson's golf spike might not have gotten wedged in between the brick and he probably wouldn't have fallen. The trial court found Larson only 49% at fault for the accident. How could Larson be held responsible for inferior con-ditions at the golf course? It was discovered that Larson had consumed 13 drinks before the accident and had a 0.29 blood–alcohol level more than 90 minutes after his fall. A doctor at the trial testified that Larson was in a stu-por, having a blood-alcohol level triple the legal limit to drive. The golf course appealed the decision, but in October 1996, Dale Larson landed in the green when the Third District Court of Appeals upheld the trial court's award of $41,000. Just another case of the court system taking a slice out of common sense.

It is against the law in Tulsa, Oklahoma, for a man to walk the streets with his shirttail hanging out.

More Legal Briefs

- The city of Los Angeles, California, announced in 1995 a $4 million overhaul of its current jury system. Included in the revamping was the issuance of mandatory thank-you notes to jurors.

- In 1995 a man who was injured in a car accident on the Golden Gate Bridge filed a lawsuit demanding that the bridge be closed.

- A 405-pound man in Portland, Oregon, sued Denny's, Inc. for $1.3 million claiming his enormous girth qualified him as "disabled," and the restaurant was ill-equipped to accommodate his special needs. The Denny's didn't have a booth or chair strong enough to support his weight, which the man claimed had made him feel like "a clown on parade."

- A couple from Berlin Heights, Ohio, sued the Natalina Pizza Company of Elyria, Ohio, in 1986 for "emotional distress" and the death of their dog. The couple claimed the expiration date on the frozen pizza they purchased was still good but the pizza looked bad. Even though they described the pizza as being "spoiled, rotten, rancid, and moldy" they had eaten several pieces and became violently ill. Pulling out of the driveway in order to rush themselves to the hospital they accidentally ran over their own dog.

It is against the law in Willowdale, Oregon, for a husband to use profane language while making love to his wife.

A Crack in the Case

Dominick and Denise Tomaselli loved their home in Bonita, California, so they were understandably upset when they discovered an inch-wide crack which appeared in the kitchen floor. They filed a claim with their insurance company, Transamerica Insurance Co., in 1988, for $170,000 to repair the floor to mint condition. The company denied their claim based on the 1987 testimony of Denise Tomaselli that a tile setter had revealed to the couple a hairline crack in the bathroom floor four years earlier. When the case went to court the Tomasellis' lawyer, Jack Winters, argued that the bathroom crack was irrelevant and unrelated to the kitchen crack. The jury agreed with the Tomasellis' lawyer and awarded the Tomasellis—in a big way. The jury found the insurance company liable for $250,000 in contract or insurance damages, $500,000 for emotional distress, and $11,250,000 in punitive damages—a total award of $12 million for an inch-wide crack. Shortly after the settlement was reached the Tomasellis were divorced; their home is now being rented out.

It is against the law in Whitehall, Montana, to drive a truck or car with ice picks attached to the wheels.

Witnessing for the Law

If you're traveling in North Miami Beach, Florida, be on the lookout for attorney R. W. Soap's place of business. Soap became a born-again Christian 14 years ago and decided to change the name of his law firm in 1993 to reflect his newly restored belief. His practice is now called the Jesus Loves You Law Office. "The main reason we picked that name is that people can know that Jesus loves them," says Soap. The Jesus Loves You Law Office accepts all types of legal cases except divorce, which Soap claims "God hates." Clients who enter Soap's firm are "handled pretty much the same as elsewhere," except Soap always asks "if they want to receive Jesus into their hearts." The name of his law office isn't the only name Soap has changed—he changed *his* name from Carlos Teplicki about a year before he renamed his law firm. According to R. W. Soap, "R. W." doesn't stand for anything, but "Soap" does: "I've been washed by the blood of Jesus, so it's a good name."

**It is against Providence, Rhode Island, law
to leap over any local bridges.**

Repellent Court

During a murder trial in Colorado, John Peters, Jr., took the stand for the prosecution as an expert witness in self-defense and aerosol chemical sprays. To visually demonstrate what Peters was talking about, prosecutor Bill Aspinwall handed him one of the exhibits, a can of aerosol bear repellent. Peters was confidently explaining how the trigger mechanism for the can of Bear-Guard worked when he accidentally squeezed the trigger, twice. The powerful spray hit the prosecutor directly in the face, and soon the entire courtroom was filled with the noxious odor. An hour later, when the court reconvened in another room, District Judge Jane Looney ruled all of Peters's testimony stricken from the record and said he could not return to the stand.

**You are allowed to kill a snake in Pennsylvania
only if the snake bites you first.**

Put It in Writing

On March 5, 1996, Tyler, Texas, District Court Judge Louis Gohmert handed down an interesting sentence to a man convicted of unauthorized use of a vehicle. Judge Gohmert could have sentenced 33-year-old Thomas Paul McDevitt to two years in state prison for stealing a car. But when the judge found out McDevitt had contracted the AIDS virus he gave him five years' probation and made his probation conditional. What was the condition? That McDevitt have all prospective sex partners sign a "consent to have sex" form which read: "Thomas Paul McDevitt has advised me that he has been diagnosed as positive for the HIV virus in his body and may be symptomatic for the disease of acquired immune deficiency syndrome. Although I realize I am potentially risking my own life, I nonetheless desire to engage in sexual relations with the above named individual."

When asked how anyone would know if McDevitt lived up to his agreement, Judge Gohmert said the conditions would be self-policing. "There's not going to be any bedroom police."

"A man shall not marry the grandmother of his wife."
—*a Kentucky statute*

Video Check-Out

Gathering evidence for a possible charge of pornography, a county detective rented four X-rated videos from a local video store. The matter was eventually dropped. The owners were in no mood to "be kind and rewind," so they decided to sue the county. They charged that the detective had returned the four porno tapes late and they sought a $3,000 settlement. The court ruled in their favor, but awarded only $64 to the store's owners—whose last name was Bible.

"Any vehicles meeting at an intersection must stop. Each must wait for the other to pass. Neither can proceed until the other is gone."
—a New Hampshire traffic ordinance

Legal Checks and Balances

William Cusack of Paterson, New Jersey, pled guilty to forgery charges on November 16, 1992, that had netted him $26,674 from a Little Falls doctor. Superior Court Judge Sidney H. Reiss sentenced Cusack to 100 days in jail with four years' probation and ordered him to make full restitution to the doctor. Cusack admitted that while serving as the office manager for Dr. Richard K. Pace, he not only illegally endorsed checks, but also wrote checks payable to himself. Cusack's lawyer, Joaquin Calcines, Jr., asked the court to go easy on Cusack because his father had died when he was a teenager, and he was helping support his mother, who was also employed by Dr. Pace. After Judge Reiss passed sentence, Calcines complained the guilty verdict would destroy Cusack's future plans. What were Cusack's career goals? Going to law school and then a career in politics.

In Santa Ana, California, a law makes it illegal for anyone to swim on dry land.

What Was Going Through Their Mind?

We've all got our reasons for doing the things we do, even if they don't make sense to other people. Here are two such stories:

• Deborah Kazuck was found guilty by a Milwaukee, Wisconsin, jury of the attempted ax murder of Jeffrey Meka. In May 1989 Kazuck had two female accomplices lure Meka to her apartment while she hid in the bathroom. When Meka went to use the toilet, Kazuck jumped at him from behind the shower curtain chanting "redrum"—murder backward, and hit Meka in the head with an ax. Meka lived. During her trial, Kazuck explained that her plan was to dismember Meka, drain his blood, and eat his kidneys. She claimed Jack the Ripper was her son in a previous life, and the ritual slaying of Meka would bring him back to life.

• In the early 1980s, a man in Virginia was convicted of second-degree murder after he chopped his mother-in-law to death with a hatchet. His defense? He said he accidentally mistook his mother-in-law for a raccoon.

It is illegal to sit on the curb of any city street in St. Louis, Missouri, and drink beer from a bucket.

The High Court

A Wisconsin prosecutor was delivering his closing arguments in a drug case and planned to use the evidence as a visual aid. One hundred dollars worth of marijuana and $580 in cash had been confiscated and marked for exhibit. But when the prosecutor went to the exhibit table to show the jury the marijuana—it wasn't there. He decided to show the jury the cash from the bust—it was missing as well. Apparently while the judge and the attorneys were conferring in chambers, the clerk had left the courtroom, the court attendant had excused himself to answer the phone, a sheriff's deputy had gone to another courtroom, the evidence had mysteriously disappeared. Even though the evidence was missing, the jurors still returned with a guilty verdict and silly smiles on their faces.

**In Alabama, it is a crime to put salt on railroad tracks.
This offense is punishable by death.**

Not Worth the Trip

In early 1995, an Oklahoma appeals court ruled that Michael Eugene Price would be granted retrials in two armed robbery cases—seems the trial judge had not explained to jurors that defendants are "presumed innocent." Price's original sentence was 32 years for the first offense and 35 years for the second. At his first retrial in March 1995, Price was once again found guilty of armed robbery, but this time he was sentenced to 60 years. In his second retrial, in October 1995, he was found guilty of the second charge of armed robbery and was sentenced to 65 years.

**In Mankato, Minnesota, it is against the law
to drive a bright red car.**

A Needling Problem

In December 1983 Wah-Ja Kim, then 58, an acupuncturist from Monterey, California, dropped by the condominium of her ex-husband, William Hall. Hall was entertaining his friend, Jeannie Westall, at the time, and Kim and Westall got into an argument. The argument turned into a fight, and during the struggle Westall allegedly bit off Kim's right pinkie finger. Shortly after that, Kim filed a lawsuit for $1 million in damages, claiming that, "She could not effectively stick pins in her patient's bodies without her little finger." Kim stated that the missing digit not only caused her financial suffering, it also caused her spiritual suffering. Kim's complaint read, "the Confucianism of her native Korea demands 'that every human being should have a perfect, whole body to join our ancestors and carry on in the next life.' " The jury was on pins and needles during the trial, but finally agreed with Kim's argument and awarded her $55,000.

In Colorado, "It is a misdemeanor for an acupuncturist to engage in sexual contact, and a felony to engage in sexual intrusion or penetration, with a patient during the course of patient care."
—Colo. Rev. Stat. § 12-29.5-108 (enacted 1989)

Don't Wake the Neighbors!!!

"No person shall halloo, shout, bawl, scream, use profane language, dance, sing, whoop, quarrel, or make any unusual noise or shout in any house in such a manner as to disturb the peace and quiet of the neighborhood."
—*a Jacksonville, Illinois, ordinance*

Unrestrained giggling while walking on city street in Helena, Montana, is forbidden by law.

A Fruitless Claim

In July 1993 Christopher Lyons, a convicted drug dealer, filed a federal lawsuit from behind prison walls for $310,000 for injuries sustained after biting into a Pop Tart. Lyons claimed the berry Pop Tart not only had a wonderful fruit filling, it also contained a sliver of glass. The then 28-year-old said the sliver injured his mouth and caused him pain, suffering, mental anguish, and "emotional trauma for loss of sleep for 72 hours, due to nightmares in which he was dead in a coffin in prison from eating Pop Tarts." In his lawsuit, Lyons named the makers of Pop Tarts, the Kellogg Company, and the J. M. Smucker Company, which supplied the fruit filling, as defendants. When the case popped up before a federal judge, he kicked the little smucker out on the grounds that Lyons failed to prove his pain and suffering reached the minimum $50,000 mark for a federal lawsuit. Now tell me this, how did a prisoner get Pop Tarts and did he have access to a toaster?

**It is against the law in Marshalltown, Iowa,
for a horse to eat a fire hydrant.**

Thy Will Be Done

In 1968 the granddaughter of Philip John Bayer, the founder of Quaker State Oil, died and left an estate worth approximately $12 million. Her will bequeathed over 1,700 pairs of shoes and 1,200 boxes of stationery to the Salvation Army. The remainder of her estate went to the dogs. Ms. Bayer, who died a spinster, had adopted 150 stray dogs as pets. Her will set up a trust fund which allowed the beasts to live like beauties for up to 20 years. At the end of the 20 years, or upon the death of the last of the mutts, whichever came first, the remainder of the estate would go to Auburn University. Finally in 1984, Musketeer, the sole survivor of the original 150 and then the richest dog in the United States, went to that great kennel in the sky. After a 16-year wait, Auburn University finally got its money.

In Tuntutuliak Village, Alaska, any dog caught in public for a second time without a leash will be shot.

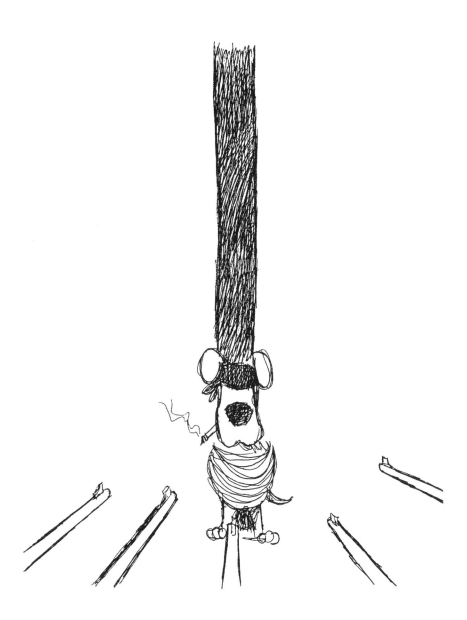

Rubbing the Judge the Wrong Way

In 1983 a lawyer was ruled to be "in contempt of court" by a judge because he had missed a court date. During his hearing on the charges, the attorney explained that he "had the screaming itches of the crotch. I wasn't here because I would have been scratching my testicles constantly." The judge was aghast at what he termed a "degrading" explanation and ruled that the lawyer's fine be doubled.

The law in Logan County, Colorado, forbids a man to kiss a woman "while she is asleep, without first waking her."

Net Profits

Jose Barretto, a student at Richmond Hill High School in New York City in 1988, decided to seize an opportunity to do some clowning around when his volleyball coach stepped out of the gym. He took a running start at the volleyball net that was some 30 feet away and attempted to leap over it. His foot caught the top of the net, and Barretto landed on the parquet floor on his head fracturing a vertebra in his neck. The accident left him paralyzed from the waist down. Barretto then filed a lawsuit against the school for failing to stop him from horsing around and eventually injuring himself. The jury was apparently sympathetic to the now wheelchair-bound youth and decided that it was the school's fault that he jumped over the net; it awarded him $18.8 million in damages. However, in March 1997, the appellate division of the New York Supreme Court called a foul on the phenomenal award. Barretto complained, "I accept part of the blame, but what about the responsibility of the teacher and the school?"

In Molie, Missouri, it is against the law to frighten a baby.

Higher Learning

Two Keene State College students agreed to have their dormitory rooms searched. The resulting search turned up Ritalin and more than six ounces of marijuana which the students had stashed away. They were arrested. In March 1996 New Hampshire Judge Philip Mangones declared the dormitory room search unconstitutional on the grounds that the two students were too stoned to know what they were doing when they consented to the search. This means the drugs can't be used as evidence in their trial. Maybe they thought the knock at the door was the pizza delivery man.

"If a stray pet is not claimed within 24 hours, the owner will be destroyed."
—an Arvada, California, ordinance

Hair Today, Gone Tomorrow

Here are some hair-raising lawsuits:

• In West Palm Beach, Florida, in 1991, Missy Freshour, then 33, arrived for her appointment at the J. C. Penney hair salon at the Palm Beach Mall. She had an appointment to have her shoulder-length light brown hair frosted. The color was applied, and Freshour was put under the hair dryer by an employee. When the employee finally came back, Freshour's hair was so badly damaged, most of it had to be cut off. She eventually had to have her hair styled like a boy's in order to cover the thin spots. In May 1992 a jury awarded Freshour $2,500 for her follicle fiasco.

• Eric S. Graham sued the J. C. Penney Co. salon at Orlando's Florida Mall for a bad haircut. Graham wanted his hair cut short on the sides and left long and curly on top. The stylist cut Graham's hair too short on top and left it long on the sides. Graham claimed the haircut deprived him of his right to enjoy life and eventually drove him to seek psychiatric treatment.

• "I sued for $2,500 and [the judge] gave me $837.29. I don't think he realizes how much a girl's hair means to her."
—*Lauryl Boyer of Castle Rock, Washington, on the award she received for a bad perm*

It is illegal to bake, for any reason, a mince pie in Beatrice, Nebraska.

Severe Penalty for Early Withdrawal

Etta Stephens of Tampa, Florida, filed a lawsuit against Barnett Bank in May 1995, seeking damages for personal suffering. Stephens's life savings, around $20,000, was in an account at Barnett Bank, and she was curious to find out how much interest her money had gained. But when she opened the envelope containing her monthly statement, she was so shocked to see a zero balance that her heart skipped a beat, literally. Stephens, statement in hand, collapsed to the floor with a heart attack. Officials at Barnett Bank apologized for the unfortunate incident and blamed the erroneous closing balance on a "printing error." No word if the bank at least gave Stephens a complimentary toaster oven for her pain and suffering.

No one is allowed to ride "an ugly horse" down the street in Wilbur, Washington. Anyone violating this ordinance could be forced to pay a $300 fine.

Vowel Play

Vanna White, the "Wheel of Fortune" co-host whose letter-turning talents have landed her a place in TV trivia history, filed a lawsuit against Samsung Electronics in 1991 claiming it used her likeness without her permission. White cited the Samsung ad, which shows a robot wearing a wig, gown, and jewelry, positioned in front of a Wheel of Fortune-like letter board. White argued that the public was likely to confuse her with the robot or think that she was associated with the advertisement. The case was appealed to the Ninth Circuit Court of Los Angeles which ruled that the robot looked a lot more mechanical than White. Circuit Judge Arthur L. Alarcon didn't need to buy a vowel when he wrote his dissent, claiming a lot of women could have filed a similar lawsuit. He wrote: "An attractive appearance, a graceful pose, blond hair, an evening gown and jewelry are attributes shared by many women, especially in southern California."

In Florida: "Whoever commits any unnatural and lascivious act with another person is guilty of a misdemeanor. A mother's breastfeeding of her baby does not violate this section."
—Fla. Stat. Ann § 800.02 (enacted 1993)

Where There's a Will, There's a Way

A person's last will and testament could be the most important legal document of his or her life. It usually contains the person's wishes, indicating who he or she likes or does not like, and which possessions he or she thinks are valuable. Check out the following wills and won'ts.

- Donald Eugene Russell, an Oregon poet, who died February 3, 1994, at 64, was refused his last wish: to have the skin removed from his corpse so it could be tanned and used as binding for a volume of his poetry. On April 4, 1994, Rachel Barton-Russell, the poet's widow, settled with the state after it filed a lawsuit halting the request. She agreed to have him cremated instead.

- Upon his death, the Chief Justice of the United States Supreme Court, Warren Burger, left a will consisting of three sentences. The will was so non-specific and vague that it could cost his heirs thousands of dollars in taxes.

- In December 1993, Anna Morgan left her entire estate, valued at $500,000, to "my best friend and companion." The recipient of the windfall is Morgan's 11-year-old Turkish Angora cat, Tinker. As a condition of the will, Morgan's Seattle apartment will be maintained through a trust fund which will also hire a live-in caretaker to look after Tinker.

It is illegal in Tennessee to catch fish with a lasso.

Reach Out and Put the Touch on Someone

A $35 million lawsuit was filed in New York State Supreme Court by Ronald Silber and his family in 1995 which named Motorola as the defendant. The Silbers claim Motorola should be held liable for the injuries they sustained when another car collided with them. The reason—the driver who injured them lost control of her car while she was reaching for a Motorola cellular phone.

A local law in North Andover, Massachusetts, prohibits its citizens from carrying what are described only as "space guns."

Not a Ghost of a Chance

The music was blaring and people were line-dancing, drinking, and having a good time at Bobby Mackey's Music World, a country music bar in Wilder, Kentucky. A patron of the establishment, J. R. Costigan, excused himself and went to the little cowboys' room. That's where he claims he was attacked. Costigan sued Bobby Mackey's in 1993 because a ghost "punched and kicked him" while he was trying to use the bar's facilities. Costigan demanded both $1,000 in damages and that a sign be prominently placed in the rest room warning innocent patrons of the ghostly presence. The lawyer for Bobby Mackey's filed a motion to have the case dismissed, citing the extreme difficulty of serving a subpoena on the ghost to testify in the trial. The case was eventually dismissed. In this case did Costigan really encounter a spirit—or did Costigan simply encounter a case of spirits?

**It is against the law in California to hunt whales
from your automobile.**

Say Cheese!

Whenever you see the Green Bay Packers playing football, you're bound to see some fans wearing big foam-rubber pieces of cheese on their heads. Wisconsin is cheese territory and residents take their fromage seriously. So seriously in fact that two makers of the cheese chapeau have taken each other to court. The original maker of the novelty hat, Foamation, Inc., has sued its cheesy rival, Scofield Souvenir Postcard Co. of Menomonee Falls, for copyright infringement, trademark infringement, and unfair competition. Scofield, who cut the cheese profits of Foamation, countersued for, among other things, tortuous interference with a business contract, libel, and defamation. It seems like there isn't enough cheese to spread around.

**It is against the law in the District of Columbia
to fly a kite.**

One for the Road

A Pontiac, Michigan, man drove his car down the wrong lane of a highway, smashed into the car driven by Sigmund and Irene Fitz, and killed them both instantly. The then 28-year-old man escaped the wreck unharmed and immediately filed suit against the Fitz's estate seeking unspecified damages. The man cried to the jury that his life had been ruined by the 1976 accident and felt he would have been better off dead. The man's attorney claimed his client should be awarded damages because Mr. and Mrs. Fitz were partially to blame since they did not swerve out of the way prior to the collision.

"Speed upon country roads will be limited to ten miles an hour unless the motorist sees a bailiff who does not appear to have had a drink in 30 days, then the driver will be permitted to make what he can."
—an El Dorado County, California, law

Just Along for the Ride

Several states have enacted car-pool or HOV (High Occupancy Vehicle) lanes to encourage people to share rides and cut down on pollution and over-crowded highways. But what constitutes High Occupancy?

• In the late 1980s, Susan Ann Yasger told an Orange County, California, judge that he should tear up the ticket given to her for driving in an HOV lane. Yasger explained that since she was pregnant, her fetus qualified as a passenger in her car, and therefore she was not breaking the law when she drove in the HOV lane. The judge agreed.

• On the other side of the coin—a 25-year-old mortuary driver was pulled over by a California Highway patrol officer and given a citation for driving alone in an HOV lane. The man appeared in court and explained to the judge that he was transporting four frozen corpses at the time and therefore wasn't traveling alone. Orange County Judge Richard Stanford, Jr., didn't buy the argument and the mortuary worker had to pay a stiff fine.

It is against the law in Winston-Salem, North Carolina, for any child under the age of seven to attend college.

Just for the Record

A slip of the tongue can happen to anyone and it's usually shrugged away or laughed off. But as a judge, everything you say is transcribed by the court reporter, and anyone can read it, over and over. A misplaced cliché can be an embarrassment, as Chief U.S. District Court Judge Oliver J. Carter knows too well. While presiding over a trial in which the defendant was a known lesbian, the judge inadvertently said, "I know you want me to put the finger in the dike for you and I'm not going to do it." And he's supposed to be up-holding the penal system!

Mississippi common law makes sure that "Every citizen has the right to shoot to kill if necessary when escorting a woman home from a quilting party and another man interferes and threatens to shoot him."

Quart Case

In 1992 Lee Outlaw was peddling his bike down a level, straight, two-lane road near Tupelo, Mississippi, when a red Ford veered out of the oncoming lane and crashed into him. The accident resulted in Outlaw suffering a badly broken leg, 1,000 stitches, and permanent scarring. Ronnie Estes, the driver of the Ford, was found to be drunk at the time of the accident. During his trial, Estes was convicted of negligent injury while intoxicated and sentenced to five years in prison. Estes appealed his sentence to the Mississippi Supreme Court; it agreed with the lower court's ruling and demanded Estes serve his time. But there was one judge, Justice Charles McRae, who disagreed with his colleagues and thought the charges against Estes should be dropped. Justice McRae's reasoning went like this: Estes's breathalyzer test showed twice the legal limit of alcohol, therefore he was too drunk to waive his right to refuse the test, and therefore the test results should have been inadmissible as evidence.

However, Justice McRae, in that opinion, also wrote: "I cannot emphasize strongly enough my abhorrence for the all-too-common practice of driving under the influence of alcohol." Two-and-a-half years after Estes's trial, Justice McRae was arrested for drunk driving after crashing his Chevy Camero into a row of trees. McRae pleaded no-contest to the charges.

**It is illegal in Youngstown, Ohio,
to ride on the roof of a taxi.**

Luck of the Irish

When Dan O'Connor, then 22, left a tattoo parlor in Carlstadt, New Jersey, he had a proud look on his face and a new tattoo on his arm. He loved Notre Dame and he decided to express his passion by spending $125 to have a tattoo of the "Fighting Irish" leprechaun permanently etched into his skin. But when he looked down to admire the tattoo artist's handiwork, he noticed something was wrong. Instead of reading "Fighting Irish" the tattoo read "Fighing Irish"—the "t" had been left out. O'Connor was "fighing" mad and he filed suit against the tattoo parlor in 1996 saying, "I can't just live with this. You're not talking about a dented car where you can get another one. You're talking about flesh." O'Connor is asking for compensation to cover the $125 cost of the tattoo and any additional costs he may accrue if he decides to have the tattoo removed with a laser. "I don't want to mangle my body. I don't want scar tissue," O'Connor lamented. "It's just my luck."

**In Washington, D.C., it's against the law
to punch a bull in the nose.**

Unfiltered Justice

Leroy Kelley, then 27, was caught red-handed stealing two packs of Marlboro cigarettes from a Safeway store in Lynnwood, Washington. When Kelley appeared in the Snohomish County courtroom before South District Court Judge Robert Schillberg in August 1993, he was expecting to have his cigarette-stealing butt kicked into jail. Judge Schillberg, however, sentenced Kelley to cough up a $1 fine and then proceeded to pay the fine out of his own pocket saying, "I think the store is more culpable than [Kelley] is" for selling such dangerous products as cigarettes. Schillberg then looked at Kelley and said, "Let's get it off your record. It's a waste of time." Other convictions on Kelley's record, but not brought up during the trial, were: shoplifting, third-degree rape, malicious mischief, assault, and resisting arrest. Sheriff's Deputy Matt Onderbeke of Snohomish County, who arrested Kelley, remarked on the judge's decision: "Do we let people off for stealing steak because it causes cholesterol problems?"

**It is illegal for monkeys to smoke cigarettes
in South Bend, Indiana.**

The Supreme Stooges

The Supreme Court took a pie in the face when a survey conducted by Luntz Research Company in Arlington, Virginia, revealed that Americans can name three of the Three Stooges more readily than three of the current U.S. Supreme Court justices. Luntz performed a nationwide telephone survey which polled 1,200 adults in early 1996, and, by a 3-to-1 margin, the Stooges beat the Supremes. Of those polled, 59 percent could name three of the six actors who at one time worked with the Three Stooges comedy trio (Moe Howard, Larry Fine, Curly Howard, Shemp Howard, Joe Besser, and Curly-Joe DeRita). Only 17 percent were able to name three of the nine Supreme Court justices—with Clarence Thomas and Sandra Day O'Connor topping the list. "The survey reflects how little the public knows about government," said Ed Miller, a Luntz senior research analyst. "It's funny, but it's kind of sad." The least known Stooge was Joe Besser and the least known Supreme Court Justice was John Paul Stevens—or did I get that backward?

**In Pacific Grove, California, it is against the law to pull
your window shades down after sunset.**

Don't Let Sleeping Dogs Lie

In July 1996 Raymondville, Texas, attorney Juan Guerra, representing Alex Alzaldua, filed a $25,000 lawsuit against Dennis Hickey. The lawsuit alleged that while at Hickey's home, Alzaldua suffered injuries when he "suddenly without warning" tripped over Hickey's dog in the kitchen. According to Guerra, Alzaldua should have been warned that he was "walking on the floor at his own risk" and of "the dog's propensity of lying in certain areas."

"No maternity hospital shall receive an infant without its mother, except in cases of emergency."
—a Colorado state statute

That Voodoo that You Do So Well

Black magic, sorcery, chants, curses, incantations, and voodoo dolls are everyday occurrences in Miami's county courthouse, so much so that an official "Voodoo Squad" has been established. The "Voodoo Squad's" responsibilities are to clean up dead chickens, goats, candles; scrub off etched symbols; and pick up charms and other ceremonial remnants each morning. A large number of the defendants on trial in Dade County are of Cuban and Haitian descent and still believe in the power of voodoo. Relatives of the accused have been caught breaking into empty courtrooms and sprinkling voodoo powder on the prosecutor's chair and the judge's bench. In one instance, during a break in a drug possession trial, two dead lizards, their mouths sewn shut with string, were found in the courtroom. Common items found around the courtroom are: eggs, which will hopefully jinx a case into collapsing; corn kernels, which help speed up a trial date; black pepper, which keeps a prisoner in jail; and cakes, which sweeten a judge's opinion of the defendant.

It is illegal in California to peel an orange in your hotel room.

Possession is Nine-Tenths of the Law

- In March 1993 Jane Bryne was in the second row of a Clayton, Missouri, courtroom observing the trial of her boyfriend, who was charged with robbing a fastfood restaurant, when her purse slipped from her grasp and fell to the floor. Detective Ron Goldstein, who was sitting in the row in front of Bryne, helped her pick up the contents and noticed, among the small cosmetic bottles, a vial filled with cocaine. "I heard change and keys rattling around and I saw lipstick and cosmetic things rolling between my feet," said Goldstein. "Then there was a bottle filled with white powder." Bryne was promptly arrested on drug possession charges.

- Two and a half years later, in Nashua, New Hampshire, during a different trial on drug possession charges, a bailiff noticed the female defendant receive a small packet from a man seated behind her. James Mascetta was quickly arrested for dispensing illegal narcotics when the packet turned out to contain heroin.

Morticians in Alabama, on threat of losing their license, are not allowed to use "profane, indecent, or obscene language in the presence of a human dead body."

Long Live the King

Elvis may be dead (or is he?), but his name lives on. On November 21, 1994, a lawsuit was filed in federal court by producer Richard Feeney, creator of the Flying Elvi. The Flying Elvi is a group of Elvis-impersonating sky divers, modeled after the team portrayed in the movie "Honeymoon in Vegas." But it was "Heartbreak Hotel" for Feeney when several members of his team broke away and formed The Flying Elvises. They did a similar Elvis-impersonated sky-diving routine and actually received a license from the Presley estate to use the name. According to Feeney's lawyer, Mark Tratos, "the team that jumped with him for two years would like to do it on their own and take over the market," which Feeney created. Feeney's suit accused the breakaway Elvises of unfair competition and trademark infringement. "That doesn't fly," responded Mark James, the Flying Elvises' lawyer. "We're the act. We would be the party that has the rights to the name." Several months later the case was settled. The Flying Elvises were forced to cease and desist their copycat performance, discontinue use of their name, and pay $80,000 to Feeney. They can, however, still say they appeared in "Honeymoon in Vegas" and are recognized by the Presley estate.

It is illegal to mispronounce the name of the city of Joliet, Illinois (it must be pronounced properly as Joe-lee-*ette*).

Spinning Out of Control

Doris Barnett of Los Angeles was selected to appear on television in the California lottery's "Big Spin" on December 30, 1995. She put her hands on the wheel, said a silent prayer, and gave the wheel a big spin. She, the studio audience, and the entire television viewing audience watched in suspense as the ball bounced around and finally settled into the $3 million slot. "Three million dollars!" shouted "Big Spin's" host Geoff Edwards as he threw his hands into the air in amazement. Soon Barnett's family charged the stage to be with their new millionaire relative, screaming, whooping, hollering, crying, and jumping in celebration. Then the ball dropped. In a pensive moment, Geoff Edwards put his hand on Barnett's shoulder and slowly turned her around to look at the big wheel. The ball had slipped out of the $3 million slot and had landed in the $10,000 slot. Edwards, with his head hung low, explained to a heartbroken Barnett that lottery rules require the ball to stay in the slot a full five seconds before a winner can be declared. Barnett and her family were quickly escorted offstage and out of sight of the studio audience. Since Barnett had been run over by the wheel of fortune, she decided to give the wheels of justice a turn and she sued the California lottery. During her trial in 1989, the jury watched video after video of other "Big Spin" contestants being declared winners even though their ball didn't stay in for the full five seconds. The jury wheeled around and awarded Barnett the $3 million that she should have won, plus an additional $400,000 for emotional trauma. The California lottery told Barnett and the jury to "spin on this" and refused to pay the award. Finally "a mutually satisfactory settlement" was reached, with the stipulation that the amount be kept a secret.

In Cottonwood, Alabama, it is against the law to have sex in a car with "flat wheels." The fine is increased if the act takes place in the backseat or while either offending party is driving the car at the time.

That's a Load of Crap

On June 5, 1989, Minnesota State Bank of St. Paul president Michael Brennan needed to relieve himself and stepped into the executive washroom of his own bank. Brennan sat on the toilet seat, completed his business, and when he flushed the toilet he nearly hit the roof. A geyser with "200 to 300 gallons" of raw sewage "came blasting up out of the toilet with such force it stood him right up," according to Brennan's attorney. Without notifying the bank, a construction company had shut off the sewer line causing pressure to build up in the pipes. Brennan sued both the city and the construction company for $50,000, citing the "humiliation and embarrassment" he suffered when his accident became public. The jury was sympathetic to Brennan's plight, but told him he was crap out of luck on any settlement. The construction company did, however, offer to buy Brennan a new suit.

"No person shall knowingly keep or harbor at his house or her house within the city any woman of ill-repute, lewd character or a common prostitute . . . other than wife, mother or sister."
—*an Ashland, Kentucky, ordinance*

Not Fit to Counterfeit

If any of these guys paid their bond in cash, I would certainly look twice before accepting it.

• In April 1992 Mario Taylor was convicted of counterfeiting and sentenced to 51 months in prison. Taylor appealed his sentence to the U.S. Court of Appeals for the Ninth Circuit, claiming the currency was produced using unsophisticated equipment. He used a common black-and-white office copier to produce the bills. The appellate court denied Taylor's claim and affirmed the lower court's ruling conviction, saying Taylor's illegal tender was "potentially passable."

• A man was sentenced to five years' probation in Baton Rouge, Louisiana, for attempting to pass counterfeit $20 bills. The currency was created by simply cutting off the corners of real $20 bills and gluing them onto the corners of $1 bills. Federal Judge John Parker called the arts-and-crafts criminal "the most inept counterfeiter I ever heard of."

It is against the law in Central Falls, Rhode Island, to pour pickle juice on trolley tracks.

Flushed With Embarrassment

Maine Superior Court Justice Francis C. Marsano walked into the bathroom of his chambers in the Machias courthouse to take care of a few things before going out and celebrating his birthday. As he shut the door to the bathroom and threw the bolt on that fateful September 8, 1993, evening, he heard an unusual sound. The pin had broken off the bolt and rattled to the floor. The justice was trapped. He didn't panic—how hard could it be to escape a bathroom? Marsano gave himself a smile of disbelief in the mirror, and that's when he saw the sign that indicated the room was a designated fallout shelter. There were no windows and the walls were made of concrete—there was no way out. The justice tried to move the bolt with a paper clip; he even removed the door's hinges, but he couldn't lift the one-and-a-half-inch-thick oak-laminated door. With a shrug the judge gave up and decided to get some sleep. "I discovered, among other things, and this is something the judiciary ought to know, that rolls of toilet paper make comfortable pillows," said Marsano. A clerk passing by the judge's chambers the next morning discovered the problem. Judge Marsano yelled to the clerk, "Get somebody to get this lock out and put on some coffee." Workers used a sledgehammer to pound on the door while others pulled at the bolt with pliers. At 8:10 AM the door opened and the judge stormed out. Twenty minutes later he was on the bench and holding court. Commenting on his 16-1/2-hour self-induced lockup, the judge said, "It puts a whole different spin on the phrase 'judicial seclusion.' "

"It is unlawful for any male person within the corporate limits of the City of Ottumwa to wink at any female person with whom he is unacquainted."

—*an Ottumwa, Iowa, municipal code*

Egg on Her Face

The children were wearing their newly purchased Easter clothes and joyfully searching for brightly colored eggs at the YMCA–sponsored Easter egg hunt in Stratford, Connecticut. Kelly Plaza, then eight, and another child spotted the same egg at the same time, and the other child pushed Kelly in order to get to the egg first. Kelly fell to the ground, and her two front teeth were knocked out during the 1994 incident. She and her father, Hector Plaza, filed suit against the YMCA on April 23, 1996, seeking damages on the grounds that the YMCA failed to provide proper supervision during the egg hunt. The girl's lawyer, Lawrence Grossman, said the girl was fitted with temporary false teeth which are noticeable and cause her embarrassment. The Plazas are suing for $15,000.

Minnesota's adultery law is great if you're a lascivious male. "Adultery occurs when a married woman has sexual intercourse with a man other than her husband, whether the man is married or not. . . . There is no prohibition against sex between a married man and an unmarried woman."
—*Minn. Stat. § 609.36 (enacted 1963)*

The Price Is Right

Janice Pennington, one of Barker's Beauties on the long-running game show "The Price Is Right," sued CBS Inc. for negligence when a television camera knocked her off stage and she broke her right shoulder. Because of the 1988 incident, Pennington missed 36 performances before returning to the show. It's difficult to gracefully display boxes of rice and "a new car!" with your arm in a sling. At the time, Pennington had been a regular hostess appearing in over 4,000 episodes in her 20 years on the daily show. On March 20, 1992, the 12-member Los Angeles Superior Court jury unanimously voted in favor of Pennington and found the network responsible. Which one of these figures did the jury think was fair for Pennington's pain, suffering, and lost wages? A) $250,000; B) $879,000; or C) $1.3 million. If you guessed "C," then "Come on down, you're the next contestant on 'The Price Is Right.'" That's right, $1.3 million for a broken shoulder. "The award is one of the largest verdicts for a fractured shoulder that I have ever heard of," said Pennington's lawyer, Lawrence Feldman. Feldman also admitted he believed that $1.2 million of the $1.3 million was for pain and suffering—the other $100,000 was for medical expenses and lost wages. If Pennington hadn't won an award, would there have been any lovely parting gifts?

All horses in Fountain Inn, South Carolina, must always, by law, wear pants in public.

Quick Convict Cases #4

- Pennsylvania inmate Rendrick Sumlin filed a $3 million lawsuit against Berks County Prison, alleging inadequate medical treatment after he was stung by a bee.

- Huntingdon State Prison inmate Warren Barrage sued for "cruel and unusual punishment" because prison officials deducted $104 from his inmate account to replace the mattress he had destroyed.

- Three inmates of the Clark County Jail in Washington filed a lawsuit claiming that Nutra-loaf, a mixture of ground vegetables, beef or chicken, apples, eggs, potatoes, etc., is "cruel and unusual punishment." The case was dismissed.

- A lawsuit filed by New York inmate and convicted murderer George Arce, allowing him to eat sesame seeds brought in by his wife, was upheld by the State Supreme Court.

- Lawrence Thompson, a Huntsville, Texas, inmate, sued for "violation of his freedom of religion." Thompson, a member of a group called the Lost-Found Nation of Islam, claims his religion doesn't allow him to wear the same clothes as women, and the unisex no-fly, no-pocket pants he was forced to wear violated that ordinance.

- A group of death row inmates in Riverbend Maximum Security Institution in Nashville, Tennessee, sued Governor Don Sundquist after he ordered their satellite dish removed. The inmates claimed satellite TV eases tension and creates a "more humane atmosphere." The governor's press secretary, Beth Fortune, stated that Sundquist "doesn't believe death row inmates should be comfortable."

In Washington State, it is against the law to pretend your parents are rich.

Please Hang Up and Try Again

In order to modernize the courthouse in Pawnee County, Kansas, in 1989, a new telephone system was installed which required the caller to punch in a personalized code before accessing long-distance numbers. Kansas District Judge C. Phillip Aldridge tried time and time again to get his call through, but he couldn't quite get a handle on the new phone system. After several aborted attempts, Judge Aldridge "reached out and touched" his phone and eight others in his suite with a saw. After the judge had systematically hacked the phones, he gathered them up and presented the jumble of plastic, wires, connectors, jacks, and receivers to the county commissioner. Accompanying the phone fragments was a check for an amount sufficient to pay for the damage and his letter of resignation. The judge was originally going to call in his resignation but . . .

"It is mandatory for a motorist with criminal intentions to stop at the city limits and telephone the chief of police as he is entering the town."
—a Tacoma, Washington, law

Law, Laws, Slaw

- It is against the law in Connecticut to sell pickles which, when dropped one foot from the ground, break or become soft. "They should remain whole and even bounce."

- In New York City "It is disorderly conduct for one man to greet another man on the street by placing the end of his thumb against the tip of his nose, at the same time extending and wriggling the fingers of his hand."

- It is a federal law that no one can throw tomatoes or eggs, rotten or not, at a member of Congress while such member is making a speech or campaigning for office. The maximum sentence for pummeling a congressperson is one year in prison and a $5,000 fine.

- In Quitman, Georgia, you'll never find out the punch line of one of the oldest jokes in the world because it's illegal there for a chicken to cross the road.

- In Altoona, Pennsylvania, it is against the law for a man to have a beard more than two feet long.

- It is illegal to throw knives at a man wearing a pin-striped suit in Natoma, Kansas.

- After dark in Geneva, New York, it is illegal to tell a gas station attendant to "fill her up!"

- "Females in heat must be properly confined so as not to entice males from home." This Maryland law omitted the fact that it was intended for female dogs.

- In Alaska it is against the law to "disturb a grizzly bear in order to take its picture."

- Mourners at funeral services held in Boston, Massachusetts, aren't allowed to take more than three sandwiches at one time.

SOURCES

Newspapers & Periodicals

ABA Journal
Associated Press
The Atlanta Constitution
The Boston Globe
Buffalo News
The Charlotte Observer
Chicago
Chicago Tribune
Citizen Patriot News Service
Esquire
The Fresno Bee (Fresno, Calif.)
Houston Chronicle
The Houston Post
Icon (Iowa City newsweekly)
Insight
Knickerbocker News
Legal Times
Liability Week
Los Angeles Daily News
Los Angeles Times
The Morning Call (Allentown, Pa.)
The Nashville Banner
Nashville Scene
National Law Journal
The New Republic
Newsday
Newsweek

The New York Times
North Jersey Herald & News
Philadelphia Daily News
The Philadelphia Inquirer
Phoenix Gazette
Pittsburgh Press
Playboy
Reader (Chicago's free weekly)
Reader's Digest
The Record (N.J.)
Rocky Mountain News
St. Louis Post-Dispatch
St. Petersburg Times
The Seattle Times
Shooting Times
Student Lawyer
Sun-Sentinel (Ft. Lauderdale, Fla.)
The Tampa Tribune
Tennessee Farm Bureau
Texas Monthly
Time
USA Today
United Press International
The Wall Street Journal
The Washington Post
The Washington Times
The Wichita Eagle
Wisconsin State Journal

BOOKS

Bathroom Readers Institute Staff. *Uncle John's Fourth Bathroom Reader.* New York: St. Martin's Press, 1991.

———. *Uncle John's Second Bathroom Reader.* New York: St. Martin's Press, 1989.

———. *Uncle John's Seventh Bathroom Reader.* Berkeley: Earth Works, 1994.

Bovard, James. *Shakedown: How the Government Screws You from A to Z.* New York: Viking Penguin, 1995.

Fortean Times Presents Strange Days #1: The Year in Weirdness. Kansas City: Andrews and McMeel, 1996.

The Guinness Book of Records: 1997 Edition. New York: Bantam Books, 1997.

Hobbie, K.R. *World's Wackiest Lawsuits.* New York: Sterling Publishing Co., Inc., 1992.

Howard, Phillip K. *The Death of Common Sense.* New York: Random House, 1995.

Hyman, Dick. *The Trenton Pickle Ordinance and Other Bonehead Legislation.* Vermont: The Stephen Greene Press, 1976.

Jones, Rodney R. and Gerald F. Uelmen. *Supreme Folly.* New York: W.W. Norton & Company, Inc., 1990.

Kirchner, Paul. *Oops! A Stupefying Survey of Goofs, Blunders, and Botches, Great and Small.* Santa Monica: General Publishing Group, 1996.

Kohut, John J. and Roland Sweet. *Dumb, Dumber, Dumbest: True News of the World's Least Competent People.* New York: NAL–Dutton, 1996.

———. *News from the Fringe: True Stories of Strange People and Stranger Times.* New York: NAL–Dutton, 1996.

Lindsell-Roberts, Sheryl. *Loony Laws & Silly Statutes.* New York: Sterling Publishing Co., Inc., 1994.

Louis, David. *2,201 Fascinating Facts.* Avenal, N.J.: Random House Value Publishing, 1988.

Machay, John "Kato." *Knuckleheads in the News.* New York: Ballantine Books, 1996.

Margolick, David. *At the Bar: The Passions and Peccadilloes of American Lawyers.* New York: Touchstone, 1995.

O'Neil, Frank. *The Mammoth Book of Oddities.* New York: Carroll & Graf, 1996.

Pelton, Robert Wayne. *Laughable Laws and Courtroom Capers: Loony Legalities and Curious Cases All Around the U.S.A.* New York: Walker and Company, 1993.

———. *Loony Laws . . . That You Never Knew You Were Breaking.* New York: Walker and Company, 1990.

———. *Loony Sex Laws That You Never Knew You Were Breaking.* New York: Walker and Company, 1992.

Posner, Richard A. and Katharine B. Silbaugh. *A Guide to America's Sex Laws.* Chicago: The University of Chicago Press, 1996.

Radelet, Michael L., Hugo Adam Bedau, and Constance E. Putnum. *In Spite of Innocence: Erroneous Convictions in Capital Cases.* Boston: Northeastern University Press, 1992

Seuling, Barbara. *It Is Illegal to Quack Like a Duck & Other Freaky Laws.* New York: Lodestar Books, 1988.

———. *You Can't Eat Peanuts in Church & Other Little-Known Laws.* New York: Doubleday, 1975.

Shepherd, Chuck. *America's Least Competent Criminals.* New York: HarperPerennial, 1993.

Shepherd, Chuck, John J. Kohut, and Roland Sweet. *News of the Weird.* New York: NAL-Dutton, 1989.

———. *More News of the Weird.* New York: NAL-Dutton, 1990.

———. *Beyond News of the Weird.* New York: NAL-Dutton, 1991.

Shook, Michael D. and Jeffrey D. Meyer. *Legal Briefs.* New York: Macmillan General Reference, 1995.

Wallenchinsky, David and Amy Wallace. *The Book of Lists.* New York: Little, Brown and Company, 1993.

White, William F. *The Lighter Side of Practicing Law: We the Lawyers* (Fourth Edition). Oregon: We, the Lawyers, 1996.